"When Will These Things Be?" Questions on Eschatology

Study Guide

BY KYLE POPE

© **Truth Publications, Inc. 2021.** All rights reserved. No part of this book may be reproduced in any form without prior written permission from the publisher. Printed in the United States of America.

ISBN 10: 1-58427-533-2

ISBN 13: 978-1-58427-533-6

Cover Photos: istockphoto.com

Truth Publications, Inc.
CEI Bookstore
220 S. Marion St., Athens, AL 35611
855-492-6657
sales@truthpublications.com
www.truthbooks.com

Table of Contents

Preface, ... 5

Introduction. 7

Big Questions
    What Is Eternal Life and Why Should It Matter to Me? 15
    What Does the Bible Teach about Hell and Who Will Go There?
    26
    Am I Ready for the End? 41

The Kingdom
    Has the Kingdom of Christ Been Established? 51
    Does the Physical Nation of Israel Still Play a Role in God's Final Plans?
    64
    Can Signs Foretell When the End Will Come? 73

Judgment Day
    What Does the Bible Teach about the Coming of Christ? 85
    What Is the Biblical Teaching on the Resurrection? 103
    Does the Bible Teach the "Rapture," the Coming of an Antichrist, and the
        Battle of Armageddon? 119

Tough Questions
    Does the Bible Teach an End of This Universe? 135
    What Is the Focus of the Mount of Olives Discourse? 149
    When Was Revelation Written and Why Does It Matter? 163

Personal Eschatology: Men's Studies
    Where Are the Dead? 179
    Does the Bible Teach Purgatory? 187
    Does the Bible Teach Reincarnation? 194

Personal Eschatology: Women's Studies
    Where Are the Dead? 203
    Does the Bible Teach Purgatory? 210
    Does the Bible Teach Reincarnation? 217

Appendix: General Studies

Does Apocalyptic Language Foreshadow or Exaggerate?
  Kyle Pope 229

Did 2020 Signal the End?
  Andrew Dow 233

Teaching a Future Judgment to the "Nones"
  David Deason 237

Is God Cruel to Send Souls to Hell?
  David A. Cox 241

Creation and the End of the World
  Jim Deason 245

"No One Knows" and the Deity of Christ
  Mike Willis 249

Is Matthew 24:34 a Transition Verse?
  Kyle Pope 253

Authors of the Essays in the Companion Text 264

Preface

He has made everything beautiful in its time. Also He has put eternity in their hearts, except that no one can find out the work that God does from beginning to end (Eccl. 3:11, NKJV).

Eschatology is the study of "end times" and the biblical events, promises, conditions, and elements associated with them. This Study Guide is designed for use with the companion volume of the same title: *"When Will These Things Be?": Questions on Eschatology* (Athens, AL: Truth Publications, Inc., 2020). At the beginning of His longest discourse on end-times events, Jesus's disciples asked Him, "Tell us, when will these things be?" (Matt. 24:3a). The studies explored in these books present the reader with similar questions in an effort to look to the Scriptures for answers to the common questions that confront us.

This Study Guide follows the essays in the companion text offering the student questions to aid in deeper study and consideration of the material. It may be used for personal or group studies. Both books begin with an Introduction surveying New Testament teaching on Christ's kingdom, then offer five categories of questions: (1) *Big Questions*, considering final reward, punishment, and preparation; (2) *The Kingdom*, its establishment, alleged relationship to modern Israel, and signs of the end; (3) *Judgment Day*, the coming of Christ, resurrection, and denominational notions taught about it; (4) *Tough Questions*, concerning the duration of the universe, scope of Jesus's teachings on "the end," and the timing of John's Apocalypse; and both conclude with (5) *Personal Eschatology*, through separate men's and women's tracks, examining the present condition of the dead and various concepts taught about it in Scripture and the religious world. Like the companion volume, this Study Guide ends with an Appendix of essays on General Studies, but the essays in this Study Guide provide the reader with seven essays not contained in the companion text.

"When Will These Things Be?" : Questions on Eschatology

It is our hope that the reader will find these books to be valuable resources to aid in the study of God's revelation on questions about "end times." Thank you for considering this material. May the Lord be glorified by its use and may the Lord bless you in the study of these important issues.

Introduction

Mark Mayberry introduces this series of studies with an overview of basic teaching on the kingdom. He takes us through essential concepts related to the kingdom, the kingdom in prophecy, preaching, and practice, and ends by considering when and where the Scriptures promised that God's kingdom would be realized.

1. How is Jesus identified in Revelation 17:14 _____
   _____

2. What are the Greek words translated "king" and "kingdom" in the New Testament? _____
   _____

3. What are six things a kingdom requires?
   1. _____
   2. _____
   3. _____
   4. _____
   5. _____
   6. _____

4. What are three realms over which Christ reigns as King?
   1. _____
   2. _____
   3. _____

5. How do Matthew 4:23 and 28:18-20 indicate to us the law that governs Christ's kingdom? _____
   _____
   _____

6. What are some ways citizens of Christ's kingdom should work to defend it? _____
   _____

"When Will These Things Be?" : Questions on Eschatology

7. What is the context of Daniel's prophecy on the kingdom in Daniel 2:44-45? _____

8. What does Isaiah 9:6-7 indicate about the duration of the Messiah's kingdom? _____

9. In the New Testament, what was the perspective of John the Baptist and Jesus regarding the kingdom? _____

10. What is a phrase that Jesus frequently used to introduce His parables? _____

11. How do the book of Acts and the apostolic epistles differ from the four gospels in their perspective on the coming of the kingdom? Offer some Scriptures to demonstrate this. _____

12. In John 18:36-37, what did Jesus affirm before Pilate? _____

13. How did Paul describe Jesus in 1 Timothy 6:15? _____

14. How does Philippians 3:17-21 identify Christians? _____

15. How does John 3:3-5 indicate that one enters the kingdom? _____

16. According to 1 Thessalonians 2:10-12, what are some duties and responsibilities of citizenship in the kingdom? _____

17. When the question, "when and where would the kingdom of God be established?" is asked, why does the perspective of the questioner affect the answer? _____

Introduction

18. Identify the perspective of the questioner indicated by each of the following phrases:
    "In that day" _____
    "At hand" _____
    "Already" _____
    "Not yet" _____
19. According to Isaiah 2:17-18, who alone will be exalted "in that day"? _____
20. What does Micah 5:1-4 say that the one born in Bethlehem would arise and do? _____
    _____

    To whom does this apply? _____
21. In Matthew 24:36, how is "that day" used in a different way than in these Old Testament texts? _____
    _____
    _____
    _____

22. Explain what John the Baptist and Jesus meant by teaching, "Repent for the kingdom of heaven is at hand" (Matt. 3:2; 4:17; 10:7; Mark 1:14-15). _____
    _____
    _____
    _____

    What does this indicate about its establishment? _____
    _____

23. List four things this teaching indicates that were needed on the part of the people:
    1. _____
    2. _____
    3. _____
    4. _____

"When Will These Things Be?" : Questions on Eschatology

24. State positively and negatively elements involved in repentance according to John's teaching in Matthew 3:4-12 and Luke 3:7-14.

Stated Positively	Stated Negatively

25. How can doubt pose a danger to our citizenship in the kingdom? _____

26. How is this illustrated in Matthew 14:28-31, and what was the solution to the problem in that passage? _____

27. How can an honest consideration of evidence help someone overcome doubt? _____

28. How is this seen in Luke 24:36-43? _____

29. How do the following Scriptures show that the kingdom was already in existence after Pentecost?
    1. Colossians 1:13-14 _____
    2. Hebrews 12:28 _____
    3. Revelation 1:6, 9 _____
    4. Revelation 5:10 _____

Introduction

30. If the kingdom now exists, how should this be reflected in the attitudes and actions of Christians? Offer Scriptures for your answers. _____
   _____
   _____
   _____

31. In 2 Timothy 4:16-18, how does Paul refer to the kingdom that distinguishes it from what he already enjoyed as a citizen of the kingdom of Christ? _____

32. In 2 Peter 1:10-11, what does Peter say will be supplied to faithful Christians in the future? _____
   _____

   What does this mean, if they were already in Christ's kingdom?
   _____
   _____

33. List six specific promises that await future fulfillment. (They each begin with the letter "r").
   1. _____
   2. _____
   3. _____
   4. _____
   5. _____
   6. _____

34. List two words used in 1 Corinthians 15 to describe the nature of the resurrection body, along with the Greek words from which they are translated and how are they defined.
   1. _____
      Greek word: _____
      Definition: _____
      _____
   2. _____
      Greek word: _____
      Definition: _____
      _____

"When Will These Things Be?" : Questions on Eschatology

35. According to Matthew 25:34, what will the righteous inherit on Judgment Day? _____

36. What is promised in Revelation 14:9-13? _____
_____

37. According to 1 Corinthians 15:20-28, following the Judgment, to whom will Christ deliver the kingdom? _____

Big Questions

What Is Eternal Life and Why Should It Matter to Me?
    Tommy Peeler

What Does the Bible Teach about Hell and Who Will Go There?
    Ron Halbrook

Am I Ready for the End?
    Bobby Graham

"When Will These Things Be?"
Questions on Eschatology

What Is Eternal Life and Why Should It Matter to Me?

   The first essay in this series was written by Tommy Peeler exploring what the Bible teaches about heaven and why all souls should desire to make it their eternal home. He begins by considering how one's beliefs about eschatology impacts life decisions, then makes the case that the promises of eternal life when fulfilled will make any amount of suffering Christians endure worth it in the end. He ends with an examination of Revelation 21 and 22, and what they tell us about heaven, concluding that eternal life will be the ultimate fulfillment of all Scripture.

1. List the three ways the word "heaven" is used in Scripture, as illustrated in this essay, and offer Scriptures demonstrating each.
   1. _____
   2. _____
   3. _____
2. In Hebrews 11:10 and 14, for what was Abraham said to be looking? _____
   According to Hebrews 11:16 what kind of place was it that he was seeking? _____
   _____
   How is it compared to earthly places? _____
3. According to Hebrews 13:14, what should Christians now seek?
   _____
   What are two ways it is described?
   1. _____
   2. _____

"When Will These Things Be?" : Questions on Eschatology

4. What is the similar complaint of those described in 2 Peter 3:3-4, Ezekiel 12:22, 27, and Jeremiah 17:15? _____
   _____

5. In 2 Peter 3:5-6, what were s scoffers overlooking? _____
   _____
   Do you think the fact that many today deny that this thing ever actually happened contributes to a denial that there will ever be a Judgment Day? _____

6. According to 2 Peter 3:8-9, why does the Lord delay? _____
   _____

7. How does 2 Peter 3:11-13 indicate that knowledge of the coming Judgment and destruction of the universe should affect our lives?
   _____

8. What do we know about the city of Philippi that provides a background for Paul's words in Philippians 3:20-21? _____
   _____
   _____

9. In what ways should citizens of the kingdom live by a different standard than those in the world around us? _____
   _____

10. What two words used in 2 Peter 2:6-8 describe Lot's attitude in seeing the wickedness of those around him?
    1. _____
    2. _____
    What does this indicate about the attitude we should have in seeing wickedness in the world today? _____
    _____
    _____

What Is Eternal Life and Why Should It Matter to Me?

11. Rather than accumulating earthly riches, what does Matthew 6:19-21 teach that Christians should "lay up"? _____
_____

12. In the parable Jesus told in Luke 12:13-34, what motivated Him to tell this parable? _____
_____

    Of what does Jesus say a person's life does *not* consist? _____
_____

13. What about the behavior of the man in the parable leads God to call him a "fool"? _____
_____

14. Have all people who have become wealthy done so by cheating and mistreating the poor? Give biblical examples to support your answer. _____
_____
_____

15. Explain what Jesus means in His command, "make yourselves money belts which do not wear out, an unfailing treasure in heaven" (Luke 12:33). _____
_____
_____
_____

16. What is the Greek word translated "soul" in Luke 12:19 and 20?
_____
    How is this word translated in Luke 12:22 and 23? _____
    Do you see any significance to this? _____
_____
_____

17. How would you answer the question posed by the author—"Are *you* living more as the rich fool than as Jesus teaches?" _____
_____
    If so, how can you change? _____
_____
_____

"When Will These Things Be?" : Questions on Eschatology

18. Summarize the Parable of the Unjust Manager in Luke 16:1-13.

    What is the main point of this parable?

19. What teaching of Jesus follows after this (Luke 16:19-31)?

    This text will be discussed quite often in the studies in this book. How does it relate to the Scriptures that came before it in Luke 16?

20. In Luke 18:18-30, what proved to be an obstacle this man's pursuit of eternal life?

    What could have helped him overcome this obstacle?

21. Explain the writer's request in Proverbs 30:8-9.

22. In 1 Timothy 6:17-19, what does Paul's phrase "the uncertainty of riches" mean?

    Where should the rich place their trust?

23. For what are the Hebrews praised in Hebrews 10:32-34?

What Is Eternal Life and Why Should It Matter to Me?

24. In the verse the author quotes from the hymn "Heaven Holds All to Me" by Tillet S. Tiddlie, what point is made about earthly treasure? _____

    Can you sing the chorus of this song in sincerity and truth? If not, what needs to change in your life? _____

25. List some of Paul's afflictions in the following passages:
    2 Corinthians 1:8-9: _____

    2 Corinthians 4:8-12: _____

    2 Corinthians 6:4-5: _____

    2 Corinthians 11:23-28: _____

    2 Corinthians 12:10: _____

26. What allowed him to describe all of these things as "momentary, light affliction" (2 Cor. 4:17)? _____

27. In 2 Corinthians 4:17, how does Paul apply the same words to the glory of eternal life that he applied to his afflictions in 1:8? _____

28. The author of this essay writes, "Far from stopping us from obtaining our goal, hardships, adversity, and persecution may actually strengthen us and help us in our journey to heaven (Rom. 5:3-5; Jas. 1:2-4)." Do you agree with this statement? Explain your answer however you answer this. _____

"When Will These Things Be?" : Questions on Eschatology

29. The author quotes Garland in saying that the goal of 2 Corinthians 4:16-5:10 is "to show how the assurance of the life to come changes everything for the Christian in the present." Read this Scripture and explain why Garland might say that. _____
_____

30. In 1 Peter 5:8-9, what does the apostle tell his readers to encourage them as they face suffering? _____
_____

31. What three ways does the author offer from 1 Peter for the Christian to overcome suffering?
    1. _____
    _____

    2. _____
    _____

    3. _____
    _____

32. Explain the author's point about the wording of Micah 5:2 and its quotation in Matthew 2:5-6 related to how Christ transforms things by His presence. _____
_____
_____

33. How does the author describe Psalm 44? _____

    Where is part of it quoted in Romans 8? _____

    How does the author explain its use in Romans 8? _____
    _____

34. Explain the author's point about Paul's use of Hosea 13:14 in 1 Corinthians 15:55-57. _____
_____

What Is Eternal Life and Why Should It Matter to Me?

35. What was Moses looking for that allowed him to endure the trials he faced (Heb. 11:26)? _____

   What is promised to those who endure persecution like the prophets (Matt. 5:12; Luke 6:23)? _____

   _____

36. In 1 Corinthians 9:24-27, to what does Paul compare the life and hope of Christians? _____

   _____

37. In the following passages, what fact about heaven does Solomon emphasize (1 Kings 8:30, 32, 34, 36, 39, 43, 45, 49, 54)? _____

   _____

38. Metonymy is a figure of speech by which something associated with a thing is referred to in place of it. Read the following Scriptures the author cites as examples of metonymy in reference to God and identify how it is used.
   Daniel 4:26: _____

   _____

   Luke 15:18: _____

   _____

   Matthew 21:25: _____

   _____

   John 3:27: _____

   _____

39. What aspect of eternal life is emphasized in John 13:33, 36-37, 14:3, and 1 Thessalonians 4:13, 17? _____

40. List how the book of Revelation describes the sea in the following passages.
   4:6: _____
   13:1-10: _____

"When Will These Things Be?" : Questions on Eschatology

17:1: _____
18:17, 19: _____
20:13: _____
How might these descriptions help us understand the figure of "no more sea" in 21:1? _____
_____
_____

41. What contrast is offered between Revelation 21:4 and passages such as Matthew 13:42, 50; 22:13; 24:51; and 25:30? _____
_____

42. The promises of Isaiah 65:17, 20, and 66:22 are similar to those of Revelation 21:4. What are some important differences? _____
_____

43. List some similarities between the vision Ezekiel sees in Ezekiel 48 and what John is shown in Revelation 21 and 22. _____
_____
_____
_____

44. List some things the author notes are indicated by the vision in Revelation 21 and 22. _____
_____
_____
_____

45. The New Testament speaks of a sense in which the Christian now sees God (1 John 3:6; 3 John 11), but also of the fact that in another sense it is impossible (1 Tim. 6:16; cf. Exod. 33:18-23). What does Revelation 22:4 promise and how does this differ from what we now enjoy? _____
_____
_____

What Is Eternal Life and Why Should It Matter to Me?

46. Explain the author's point that heaven will be the answer to the problem of sin. _____
_____
_____

47. In Revelation 22:1-5, identify the elements associated with the Garden of Eden mentioned in the following texts.
    Genesis 2:9; 3:22: _____
    Genesis 2:10-14: _____
    Genesis 3:14, 17: _____

48. What does Hebrews 11:8-16 teach about Abraham's hope in heaven? _____
_____
_____
_____

49. Read Hebrews 3:7-4:11. How does this passage relate the Promised Land of Canaan to eternal life with God in heaven? _____
_____
_____
_____

50. After what does the author argue that the seven trumpets of Revelation 8:1-11:9 and bowls of wrath in Revelation 16 are patterned? Explain his argument. _____
_____
_____
_____

51. In what ways will heaven be a fulfillment and parallel to the Israelites' exodus from Egypt? _____
_____
_____
_____

"When Will These Things Be?" : Questions on Eschatology

52. What description from Psalm 2 is applied to Christ's reign in Revelation 12:5 and 19:15? _____

53. In Galatians 4:22-26, how is heaven described in relation to "Jerusalem which now is"? _____

54. To what does Hebrews 12:22-24 say Christians have come? _____

    Does this mean that Christians now enjoy all that this "heavenly Jerusalem" has to offer? Why or why not? _____

55. What are some promises made in Isaiah that are fulfilled in heaven?
    _____
    _____
    _____

56. How does the book of Ecclesiastes build the argument that life on earth is ultimately meaningless? _____

    How does heaven overcome this? _____

57. Read the following passages the author offers in which God's relationship to His people is described as a marriage: Isaiah 54:5; Jeremiah 3:1-11; Hosea 1-3. In the New Testament this image is used in Mark 2:19-22; Matthew 22:1-14; 25:1-13; John 3:29; 2 Corinthians 11:2; Ephesians 5:25; Revelation 19:7-9; 21:2, 9. How will eternal life in heaven be a fulfillment of this? _____

What Is Eternal Life and Why Should It Matter to Me?

58. What is a fact about the tabernacle or temple that is often emphasized? _____
    How does Revelation 21:3 relate this to heaven? _____
    _____
    _____

59. Explain the author's argument that heaven is the fulfillment of the tabernacle or temple in the Old Testament. _____
    _____
    _____
    _____
    _____

60. How are the twenty-four elders of Revelation 4:4 and 10 generally identified (cf. Rev. 21:12-14)? _____
    _____
    What other possible interpretation does the author offer? _____
    _____
    _____
    _____

61. According to Revelation 21:7, who will inherit the things described? _____

62. How do the following Scriptures describe Jesus?
    John 10:1-18: _____
    John 4:10, 13-14: _____
    John 6:35: _____
    How will eternal life in heaven be a fulfillment of these descriptions (cf. Rev. 7:16-17; 21:6; 22:17)? _____
    _____
    _____
    _____

What Does the Bible Teach about Hell and Who Will Go There?

The second essay considering "Big Questions" was written by Ron Hallbrook on the question of eternal punishment. After surveying biblical evidence for hell throughout the entirety of Scripture, the author offers refutation of the doctrine of annihilationism: the belief that souls unworthy of heaven pass out of existence.

1. What is the context of Matthew 13:41-42? _____

   What does Jesus say will happen to those described as "tares" in the parable and explanation just before these verses? _____

2. Explain the author's illustration about oil and water and the need for a place of eternal punishment. _____

3. How does Genesis 18:23 and 25 illustrate this point? _____

4. How does Deuteronomy 4:24 describe God? _____

   Explain what this means? _____

   Relate this to Deuteronomy 7:9-10. _____

What Does the Bible Teach about Hell and Who Will Go There?

5. In a footnote, the author quotes Edward Fudge, who advocated a view that hell is punishment and then annihilation. Explain the point the author makes about the weakness of this view to satisfy the charges of critics regarding any concept of hell. _____
   _____
   _____

6. List two lies the author suggests Satan has told from the beginning, as illustrated from Genesis 3:4-5.
   1. _____
   _____
   2. _____
   _____
   How has our world fallen pray to these lies?_____
   _____
   _____

7. What does the common phrase "died, and was gathered unto his people" (Gen. 25:17; 35:29; 49:33; et al.) infer about the soul's existence after death? _____
   _____

8. Explain the author's argument that giving man an eternal soul and the freewill to choose whether to sin necessitates the creation of a place to separate eternally those who sin from the presence of God.
   _____
   _____
   _____

9. What does 1 Peter 3:19-20 say about the present condition of those who died in the Flood?_____
   _____
   _____
   _____

27

"When Will These Things Be?" : Questions on Eschatology

10. What is the name of the portion of hades where angels who sinned are presently bound (2 Pet. 2:4)? _____
    How does the King James Version translate this name? _____
    How do we know this place is not the place of final punishment?
    _____
    _____

11. How does Matthew 11:23-24 demonstrate that the destruction of Sodom points to a final judgment in hell? _____
    _____

12. Read Psalm 16 and note elements within it that infer the hope of eternal life for the righteous and promise of eternal punishment for the wicked beyond the grave. _____
    _____
    _____

13. Explain the author's interpretation of the phrase "blotted out their name for ever and ever" in Psalm 9:5-6. _____
    _____
    _____

14. In Psalm 69:27-28, what does the reference to names being "written" in a "book" indicate about what will happen to souls at some point after death? _____
    _____

15. What does Psalm 73 indicate about hell? _____
    _____

16. What rhetorical questions are asked in Isaiah 33:14? _____
    _____
    _____
    _____

What Does the Bible Teach about Hell and Who Will Go There?

Do you think this teaches anything about eternal punishment? Why or why not? _____
_____
_____

17. If Isaiah promises that the wicked will have "no peace" (Isa. 48:20-22; 57:1-2, 15, 19-21), what does that indicate about eternal life and the longevity of the soul? _____
_____
_____

18. What terminology later used in the New Testament of hell is found in Isaiah 66:24? Explain its usage in this text. _____
_____
_____
_____

19. What does Daniel 12:2 teach about the ultimate fate of the wicked? _____
_____

Advocates of the AD 70 Doctrine claim this is talking about what happened in the Roman destruction of Jerusalem. Explain the author's interpretation of the context and promise of this passage.
_____
_____
_____
_____

20. What three prerequisite truths to the doctrine of hell as eternal punishment does the author point out that Jesus taught?
    1. _____
    2. _____
    3. _____
    _____

"When Will These Things Be?" : Questions on Eschatology

21. In a footnote, how does the author refute the dismissal of the force of Luke 16:19-31 by the Jehovah's Witnesses claim that it is only a parable? _____
_____
_____

22. What is the Greek word translated "hell" and from what is this name drawn? _____
_____

    In the Old Testament, what happened in this place? _____
_____
_____

    How many times does Jesus use this word in reference to eternal punishment? _____

23. In Matthew 18:5-9, what does Jesus teach would be better for a person to suffer than to cause someone to sin? _____
_____

    What does this tells us about the nature of eternal punishment?
_____
_____

24. How is hell described in Mark 9:42-48? _____
_____

    What does this indicate about its duration? _____
_____

25. What does Jesus teach in Matthew 10:28? _____
_____

    What is the Greek word translated "destroy" in this verse and what does it mean? _____
_____

What Does the Bible Teach about Hell and Who Will Go There?

How is this destruction described in the parallel text in Luke 12:4-5? _____
_____

26. Explain Jesus's reference to hell in Matthew 23:15. _____
_____
_____

27. What word in Greek is used to describe hell in Matthew 7:13 and how is it translated? _____

    How does the use of the same word in Matthew 26:8 help us understand its meaning? _____
_____

28. How is hell described in Matthew 8:12? _____
_____

29. List the descriptions of hell found in the following passages.
    Matthew 13:41-42: _____

    Matthew 13:49-50: _____

    Matthew 24:45-51: _____

30. Explain the meaning of the phrase "outer darkness." _____
_____
_____
_____

    How often does Jesus describe hell in this way? _____
31. Compare the wording of the demons as recorded in Mark 1:24 and Matthew 8:29. In Matthew, what phrase stands parallel to the phrase "destroy us" in Mark? _____
_____

"When Will These Things Be?" : Questions on Eschatology

What does this tell us about the meaning of the word "destroy"?

32. How is hell described in Matthew 25:40-46? _____

33. In Matthew 25:46, what is the Greek adjective modifying both the word "life" and "punishment"? _____
    Explain the author's quote from Robertson, "If the punishment is limited, *ipso facto* the life is shortened." _____

34. What are the two types of resurrection promised in John 5:25-29. Explain the meaning of both. _____

35. In Romans 2:5, 8-9, and 12, what does Paul teach about eternal judgment? _____

36. In the author's quote from Lenski, explain the argument against the charge that God is "cruel and bloodthirsty." _____

37. According to 2 Corinthians 5:10-11, what should a recognition of the inevitability of judgment lead a Christian to do? _____

38. Define the following types of death.
    Physical death: _____

What Does the Bible Teach about Hell and Who Will Go There?

Spiritual death: _____

39. Explain what Paul means by teaching that Christ "abolished" death in 2 Timothy 1:10. _____
_____
_____

40. Read 2 Thessalonians 1:4-10 and list every element you find that defines the nature of eternal punishment. _____
_____
_____

Advocates of the AD 70 Doctrine argue that this is only describing what happened in the destruction of Jerusalem. Do you see things in the text that refute this argument? _____
_____
_____

41. Read Hebrews 10:26-31 and make note of what it says about the fate of those who return to sin. _____
_____
_____

42. How can we know that the word "death" in James 1:13-15 and 5:20 is not discussing physical death? _____
_____
_____

43. What does James 3:6 tach about the tongue and hell? _____
_____

Explain this. _____
_____
_____

"When Will These Things Be?" : Questions on Eschatology

44. What do 2 Peter 2:1-10 and 2:20-21 teach about hell? _____
   _____
   _____

45. What does Jude 6-7 teach about the inhabitants of Sodom? _____
   _____

   What does this indicate about hell? _____
   _____
   _____

46. Read the following Scriptures and make note of how each describes the fate of the wicked after judgment.
   Revelation 2:10-11: _____
   _____

   Revelation 20:6-15: _____
   _____
   _____

   Revelation 21:8:_____
   _____

47. In the author's quote from King, what do we see in Revelation 6:10 that support's King's assertion that it demonstrates "the conscious existence of the soul after death"? _____
   _____

48. Read the following passages that also use the Greek word *diaphtheirō*, translated "destroy" and "destroying" in Revelation 11:18. What do these passages teach us about the meaning of the word? Does it mean to annihilate?
   Luke 12:33:_____
   _____

34

What Does the Bible Teach about Hell and Who Will Go There?

1 Timothy 6:5: _____
_____
_____

49. Read Revelation 14:10-11 and make note of what it teaches about eternal punishment of the wicked. _____
_____
_____

    Does this text support the doctrine of universalism or annihilation? Why or why not? _____
_____
_____

50. In Revelation 19:20, what is the fate of the "beast" and the "false prophet"? _____
_____
_____
_____

    If these in any way represent human being, what does it indicate about the fate of the wicked? _____
_____
_____

51. Hailey would later accept annihilationism, but explain the force of his argument against it in the author's quote from him in his commentary on Revelation. _____
_____
_____
_____
_____

52. What does Revelation 22:15 say about the fate of the wicked after judgment? _____
_____

    What are some inescapable conclusions we can draw from what is said? _____
_____
_____
_____

"When Will These Things Be?" : Questions on Eschatology

53. Who could be considered the first to deny the reality of hell (Gen. 3:4)? _____

54. What were some doing in the time of Jeremiah (Jer. 6:11, 14)? _____

55. What are the two "main lines of thought" that argue against conscious eternal torment in hell?
    1. _____
    2. _____

56. Explain the author's statement that "hell manifests both the love and the justice of God." _____

57. How does Matthew 22:31-32 address the question of whether the soul survives the death of the body? _____

58. List the eleven consequences the author offers if death is annihilation.
    1. _____
    2. _____
    3. _____
    4. _____
    5. _____
    6. _____
    7. _____
    8. _____

What Does the Bible Teach about Hell and Who Will Go There?

9. _____

10. _____

11. _____

59. Explain the author's argument that annihilationism make the biblical teaching on hell identical to the concept of Nirvana taught in Buddhism or Hinduism. _____

60. How does the claim of Jesus in John 8:58 demonstrate that Jesus never ceased to exist (cf. Exod 3:14)? _____

    Explain the author's quote from Barrett. _____

61. How does John 5:28-29 refute the teachings of both universalism and annihilationism? _____

    How do advocates of the AD 70 try to explain John 5:28-29? _____

62. How does Matthew 25:46 refute the concept of annihilationism?

"When Will These Things Be?" : Questions on Eschatology

Explain the significance of the author's quote from Stuart regarding this passage? _____
_____
_____

63. The author discusses three men associated with churches of Christ who began to teach annihilationism. List the men's names and their books in which this doctrine was promoted.
    1. Name: _____
       Book: _____
    2. Name: _____
       Book: _____
    3. Name: _____
       Book: _____
    How do each of these men explain Matthew 25:46? _____
    _____
    _____
    _____

64. Explain the author's assertion, "the cessation of punishment is *not* punishment." _____
    _____
    _____
    _____

    Do you agree with this statement? Why or why not? _____
    _____
    _____

65. How might arguments that remove the concept of duration from the adjectives "everlasting" or "eternal" ultimately lead one to abandon belief in God? _____
    _____
    _____
    _____

What Does the Bible Teach about Hell and Who Will Go There?

66. List the three lessons the author suggests are emphasized by the reality of hell.
    1. _____
       _____
    2. _____
       _____
    3. _____
       _____

67. How does 1 Timothy 5:6 describe those who live in sin? _____
    _____

68. How is every sin a "heinous insult to God"? _____
    _____
    _____

69. How is hell described in Revelation 21:8? _____
    _____

    Who is said to go there? _____
    _____

70. Explain how Romans 5:20-21 demonstrate what the author describes as "God's super-abundant grace"? _____
    _____
    _____
    _____

71. Whom does 2 Thessalonians 1:7-10 teach will be lost in hell? ____
    _____
    _____

72. Will more people be saved or lost (Matt. 7:13-14)? _____
    _____

73. According to Jesus, what will be the fate of that which God has not "planted" (Matt. 15:8-14)? _____
    _____
    _____

"When Will These Things Be?" : Questions on Eschatology

74. When Simon sinned, what was he told (Acts 8:20-22)? _____
    _____
    What does this teach us about the consequences of unrepentant sin in the life of a Christian?_____
    _____
    _____
    _____

75. According to 1 John 2:2, what has God offered so that any soul who accepts it need not suffer eternal punishment?_____
    _____
    _____

76. How does John 5:24 teach that one may "not come into condemnation"?_____
    _____

Am I Ready for the End?

The final essay examining "Big Questions" was written by Bobby Graham. If we understand that heaven or hell are the final destinations for all souls, the question we each must ask is, "Am I ready for the end?" After demonstrating its reality and defining the meaning of "the end," this study explores a series of questions drawn from events that will happen on the "Last Day." Understanding what Scripture teaches about this day should challenge each of us to "Prepare to meet your God" (Amos 4:12).

1. How do the mottoes of the Boy Scouts and the United States Coast Guard illustrate the value we place on readiness in physical things? _____
   _____
   Is readiness in spiritual matters any less important? _____
2. How would you honestly answer each of these questions right now?
   "Am I ready to die?" _____
   "Am I ready for the Lord to return?" _____
   "Am I ready to face the Lord in judgment?" _____
   If you answered "no" to any of these questions, what should you do to get ready? _____
3. What are some things you have done to prepare to:
   Start school? _____
   _____
   Find a job? _____
   _____
   Start a family? _____
   _____
   Buy or sell a house? _____
   _____

"When Will These Things Be?" : Questions on Eschatology

Raise your children? _____

_____

These are important things, but what preparation have you made for eternity? _____

_____

4. According to Matthew 24:36, can human beings know when Judgment Day will come? _____

_____

5. In John 5:28-29, list some things Jesus says will happen one day.

_____

_____

_____

6. List some of the "ends" that some look to rather than a future Second Coming of Jesus to raise and judge all. _____

_____

_____

_____

Why do you think some deny that Jesus one day will actually return to judge the world? _____

_____

_____

7. Read 1 Corinthians 15:24-28. List some things found in this text which demonstrate that the "ends" listed in number 6 could not be the "end" of which Paul speaks. _____

_____

_____

_____

_____

8. Explain the saying, "time is a parenthesis between two eternities" and offer Scripture to demonstrate its accuracy. _____

_____

_____

_____

_____

Am I Ready for the End?

9. What does 2 Peter 3:9 teach us about God's attitude towards time?
   _____
   _____
   _____

   Full-preterists like to argue, "God knows how to keep time," then insist that "quickly" and "soon" must indicate fulfillments in the first century. How would you answer this in light of 2 Peter 3:9? _____
   _____
   _____

10. In this essay, the author writes, "An eternal God does not perceive of different measures of time the same as finite man. He simply is not bound by time!!" Do you agree with these statements? Why or why not? _____
    _____
    _____

11. Some argue the "last day" consists of 1000 years, just as some argue the "first day" lasted millions of years. From Scripture, how would you refute both claims? _____
    _____

    Are there similar mindsets that lead people to these conclusions? What similarities do they share in common? _____
    _____
    _____
    _____

12. List the six things identified in this study that will take place on the "Last Day."
    1. _____
    2. _____
    3. _____

"When Will These Things Be?" : Questions on Eschatology

    4. _____
    5. _____
    6. _____

13. When does John 6:40 say God will *raise up* those who will receive everlasting life? _____

14. Describe all that is said in 1 Corinthians 15:51-52 about what happens when "we shall all be changed." _____
_____
_____
_____

15. What argument does the author make to show that 1 Thessalonians 4:16 cannot be interpreted to mean that the wicked will be resurrected 1,000 years after the righteous? _____
_____
_____

16. When Jesus returns, what does 1 Thessalonians 4:13-17 say will happen to those who "are alive and remain" when He comes? _____
_____
_____

17. In 2 Timothy 4:8, what does Paul mean in speaking of those who "have loved His appearing"? _____
_____
_____

18. Under what circumstances might someone be "ashamed before Him at His coming" (1 John 2:18)? _____
_____
_____
_____

Am I Ready for the End?

19. Some have argued that Matthew 25:31-32 is describing what happened in AD 70 when Rome destroyed Jerusalem. What do you see in the wording of this text that refutes that idea? _____
   _____
   _____
   _____

20. In each of the following Scriptures, whom does each passage indicate will be present at the Final Judgment?
    Matthew 25:31-32: _____
    Matthew 12:41: _____
    Matthew 12:42: _____
    Matthew 11:20-24: _____
    2 Thessalonians 1:6-10: _____
    2 Corinthians 5:10: _____

21. Some teach that when Jesus returns, the universe will not be destroyed but rejuvenated and renewed. List some of the words and phrases used in 2 Peter 3:10-13 that refute this idea. _____
    _____
    _____
    _____

22. Advocates of the AD 70 Doctrine argue that 2 Peter 3:10-13 is describing the end of the Jewish System, not the physical heavens and earth. Read all of chapter three and list each time "heaven" and "earth" are referenced then identify whether it is describing the material universe or not. Discuss what this context indicates about their argument. _____
    _____
    _____
    _____

23. According to 1 Corinthians 15:24-26, what will Christ do to the kingdom when He returns? _____
    _____

"When Will These Things Be?" : Questions on Eschatology

Since the church is Christ's kingdom, what must this indicate about the Headship of the church now—if Christ has already come (as preterists claim)? _____
_____
_____

24. If you and I are not ready for Christ's return, will this cause Him to delay His coming? _____
_____

How does the childhood game "Hide and Seek" illustrate what we will face on Judgment Day? _____
_____
_____

25. In Matthew 24:36-42, what comparison does Jesus make to the time of Noah and His Second Coming? _____
_____

26. Explain Paul's statement in 1 Thessalonians 5:1-8 that Jesus will return "as a thief in the night." _____
_____

27. In 1909, James H. Stanley wrote a hymn drawn from the wording of Hosea 4:12 entitled, "Prepare to Meet Thy God." Lookup and read the lyrics to this hymn. What are some important points it makes about the need for preparation? _____
_____

28. In Matthew 26:41, what does Jesus urge His disciples to do lest they "fall into temptation"? _____
_____
_____

Am I Ready for the End?

29. What does 1 Peter 4:7 say is "at hand" and what did Peter command his readers to do because of this? _____
   _____
   _____
   _____

   What does the author say that Hamilton argues about the meaning of "at hand" here? _____
   _____
   _____

30. How does the author explain the meaning of the word "scarcely" in 1 Peter 4:18? _____
   _____
   _____

   How do 1 Peter 4:12 and 16 support this interpretation? _____
   _____
   _____

31. According to 2 Thessalonians 1:3-10, what can a person do to be prepared for the coming of Christ? _____
   _____
   _____
   _____

   What does it teach are the consequences of being unprepared?
   _____
   _____
   _____

47

The Kingdom

Has the Kingdom of Christ Been Established?
   Joe Price

Does the Physical Nation of Israel Still Play a Role in God's Final Plans?
   Stephen Russell

Can Signs Foretell When the End Will Come?
   Allen Dvorak

"When Will These Things Be?"
Questions on Eschatology

Has the Kingdom of Christ Been Established?

To begin the series of essays on the kingdom, Joe Price addressed the question of whether the kingdom has been established. Considering biblical teaching on its approach and identity along with Old Testament prophecies foretelling its coming, the essay concludes by examining New Testament texts that prove its establishment in the first century.

1. What did Gabriel tell Mary about the kingdom over which her Child would reign (Luke 1:32-33)? _____
   _____

2. What was Joseph told about Jesus (Matt. 1:20-23)? _____
   _____

   What had Isaiah said that Joseph was told would be fulfilled in Jesus (Isa. 7:14)? _____
   _____

3. How is the gospel described in the preaching of Jesus (Matt. 4:23; 9:35)? _____
   _____

4. What had Jesus declared about the coming of the kingdom and those who heard Him preach (Mark 9:1)? _____
   _____

   If it did not come in the first century what would this indicate about Jesus and His teaching? _____
   _____
   _____
   _____

"When Will These Things Be?" : Questions on Eschatology

5. What does premillennialism teach about the kingdom? _____
   _____
   _____

   Illustrate this from the author's quote of the premillennialist named Pentecost. _____
   _____
   _____

6. In this view what is the relationship between the kingdom of Christ and the church of Christ? _____
   _____

7. What does realized eschatology (or the AD 70 Doctrine) teach about the kingdom? _____
   _____
   _____
   _____

8. What event does the author argue constituted the establishment of the church and the kingdom? _____
   _____
   _____

   What does he argue is the relationship between the church and the kingdom? _____
   _____

9. What is the Hebrew word translated "kingdom"? _____
   How is it defined? _____
   _____
   _____
   _____

10. What is the Greek word translated "kingdom"? _____
    How is it defined? _____
    _____
    _____
    _____

Has the Kingdom of Christ Been Established?

11. Read Isaiah 9:6-7 and note some things it says about the kingdom over which the Messiah would reign. _____
_____
_____
_____

12. What do the following passages say about the nature of the kingdom?
    Hebrews 1:8-9: _____
    _____
    _____
    Hebrews 12:28: _____
    _____

13. List three facts the author asserts about the identity of the kingdom.
    1. _____

    2. _____

    3. _____

14. What did Jesus tell Pilate when He was asked if He was a king (John 18:37)? _____
    _____

15. How does Jesus use the terms "church" and "kingdom" interchangeably in Matthew 16:18-19? _____
    _____

16. Explain the connection the author makes between Daniel 7:13-14 and Ephesians 1:20-23. _____
    _____
    _____

"When Will These Things Be?" : Questions on Eschatology

17. What does Colossians 1:13-14 say about the present status of Christians? _____
   _____

   What does this indicate about whether the kingdom has already been established? _____
   _____

18. What did Jesus preach about when the kingdom would be established (Mark 1:14-15)? _____
   _____

19. What did Jesus teach about the nature of His kingdom (John 18:36-37)? _____
   _____

20. Following Jesus's resurrection, what does Luke say He explained to His disciples (Luke 24:44-47; cf. Acts 1:2-3)? _____
   _____
   _____

21. What did John the Baptist teach about the establishment of the kingdom (Matt. 3:2; 10:7; Mark 1:14-15; Luke 10:9)? _____
   _____
   _____

22. Explain Jesus's words in Luke 16:16. _____
   _____

   This was prior to Pentecost. In what sense were people "pressing into" the kingdom? _____
   _____

23. Read Luke 17:20:21 and list some facts it states about the kingdom.
   _____
   _____
   _____

Has the Kingdom of Christ Been Established?

24. What did Philip teach the Samaritans (Acts 8:12)? _____
_____

25. What did Paul teach in Ephesus (Acts 19:8-10)? _____
_____
_____

26. When he was taken to Rome, what did Paul teach (Acts 28:23, 28, 30)? _____
_____

    What link exists between forgiveness of sins and the kingdom?
    _____
    _____

27. What was David promised in 2 Samuel 7:12-14? _____
_____
_____

28. How does Acts 2:33-36 demonstrate that Jesus now reigns over His kingdom? _____
_____
_____

    Can there be a king without a kingdom? _____
    How does this refute both premillennialism and realized eschatology? _____
    _____

29. Read Psalm 2 and note some things it says about the Messiah and His reign. _____
_____
_____
_____

"When Will These Things Be?" : Questions on Eschatology

30. How do the following Scriptures that reference Psalm 2 apply it to Jesus?

    Acts 4:25-28: _____

    _____

    Acts 13:32-33: _____

    _____

    Hebrews 1:5: _____

    _____

    Hebrews 5:5: _____

    _____

    Revelation 2:26-27: _____

    _____

    Revelation 12:5: _____

    _____

    Revelation 19:15-16: _____

    _____

31. Read Isaiah 2:2-5. When did this happen (cf. Luke 24:44-47)?_____

    _____

    _____

    When does Acts 2:16-17 identity as the "last" or "latter" days?

    _____

    _____

32. From the author's quote from Mayberry, list several things Isaiah prophesied about the kingdom and supply the Scriptures cited.

    _____

    _____

    _____

    _____

33. Explain the author's exposition of Joel 2 and its promises regarding the kingdom._____

    _____

    _____

Has the Kingdom of Christ Been Established?

How are these things fulfilled in the New Testament? _____
_____
_____
_____

34. Explain the author's exposition of Daniel 2 and its promises regarding the kingdom. _____
_____
_____

    How are these things fulfilled in the New Testament? _____
    _____
    _____

35. How does the phrase "in the days of these kings" in Daniel 2:44 indicate when the kingdom would be established? _____
    _____
    _____

36. Read the following passages and note what they say about the Messiah and the kingdom. Make note of New Testament passages that fulfill the promises of each text.
    Psalm 110: _____
    _____
    _____

    Isaiah 9:6-7: _____
    _____
    _____

    Isaiah 11: _____
    _____
    _____

    Daniel 7:13-14: _____
    _____
    _____

"When Will These Things Be?" : Questions on Eschatology

Zechariah 6:12-13: _____

_____

Zechariah 9:9-10: _____

_____

37. List four things the author notes that Jesus said about the approach of the kingdom.
    1. _____
    2. _____
    _____
    3. _____
    _____
    4. _____

38. What did Jesus say about the kingdom in Mark 1:14-15? _____

    _____

    What does the phrase "at hand" mean? _____

    _____

    What does this indicate about when the kingdom would come?

    _____
    _____

39. What did Jesus say about the kingdom in Luke 16:16? _____

    _____

    Explain this passage and what it indicates about the existence of the kingdom. _____

    _____

40. Read these passages and note what each says about the kingdom.
    Matthew 6:10: _____

    _____

    Mark 12:34: _____

    _____

    Luke 12:32: _____

    _____

Has the Kingdom of Christ Been Established?

If the kingdom did not come until AD 70 (as realized eschatology teaches) or it still has not come (as premillennialism teaches) how does that contradict the teaching of these passages? _____
_____

41. What did Jesus say that His miracles indicated (Matt. 12:28; Luke 11:20)? _____

42. What phrases are used interchangeably in Matthew 13:11 and Mark 4:11 and in Matthew 13:31-32 and Mark 4:30-31? _____
_____

43. What did Jesus say some would see before they tasted death (Mark 9:1).? _____

44. In Acts 1:13, what did Jesus discuss with His disciples? _____
_____

45. With what did Jesus say the apostles would be "endued" "not many days" from when He spoke to them (Luke 24:48-49; Acts 1:4-6)?
_____

    What did He say they would receive when the Holy Spirit came upon them (Acts 1:7-8; John 14:26; 15:26-27; 16:8-13)? _____
_____

46. On Pentecost, what did the apostles preach about Christ's reign and power (Acts 2:30-36; Psa. 110:1-2)? _____
_____
_____

    How does this demonstrate the establishment of the kingdom at that time? _____
_____
_____

"When Will These Things Be?" : Questions on Eschatology

47. If the kingdom did not come within the lifetime of those to whom Jesus spoke in Mark 9:1, what does it make Jesus (cf. Deut. 18:20)? _____

48. What five truths about the nature of the kingdom does the author offer?
    1. _____
    2. _____
    3. _____
    4. _____
    5. _____

49. If the kingdom was to come through military conquest, what does John 6:15 record about how Jesus discouraged this concept? _____

50. How does Matthew 22:15-22 show that Jesus did not intend to establish a political and nationalistic kingdom? _____

51. What does Galatians 3:28 teach about the ethnic makeup of the kingdom? _____

52. List six points the author offers as evidence that Christians currently participate in the kingdom.
    1. _____
    2. _____
    3. _____
    4. _____
    5. _____
    6. _____

Has the Kingdom of Christ Been Established?

53. How does Acts 28:28-31 demonstrate that salvation and preaching the kingdom of God are inseparable? _____
_____
_____
_____
_____

54. How does 1 Peter 2:9 describe the church? _____

   What is the Greek word translated "royal" and what does it mean?
   _____
   _____

   How does its use in this text demonstrate the kingdom's present existence? _____
   _____
   _____

55. According to Revelation 5:10, what has God made Christians? (Note how a few different translation render this verse.) _____
_____
_____
_____

56. In Revelation 1:9, in what does John tell his readers he was a companion with them? _____

57. Read Matthew 26:29 and 1 Corinthians 10:16-17. Explain what these texts teach about the connection between the eating of the Lord's Supper and the kingdom. _____
_____
_____
_____

"When Will These Things Be?" : Questions on Eschatology

58. Explain the points the author makes about the problem the previous passages pose to believers in the AD 70 Doctrine. _____
_____
_____
_____

59. What does Paul teach in Philippians 3:20? _____
_____

60. In 1 Corinthians 15:24-26, what does Paul teach about the kingdom when "the end" comes? _____
_____
_____

    What does this indicate about the present existence of the kingdom?
_____
_____

61. List the five points the author offers to demonstrate that gospel preaching is kingdom preaching.
    1. _____
    _____
    2. _____
    3. _____
    _____
    4. _____
    5. _____

62. What does Ephesians 1:20-23 teach about the authority Jesus possessed when Paul wrote that epistle? _____
_____
_____

    How does that demonstrate the kingdom's existence? _____
_____
_____
_____

Has the Kingdom of Christ Been Established?

63. What did Philip preach in Acts 8:12? _____
_____

64. In the following passage how does the accusation of enemies of the gospel demonstrate the existence of the kingdom?
Acts 17:7: _____
_____
_____

65. Compare Hebrews 12:28 and Daniel 2:44. Since the Hebrew writer describes a present condition, what does that indicate about the existence of the kingdom when the book was written? _____
_____
_____

66. What does Revelation 12:10 declare? _____
_____
_____

According to John 12:31-33 and Hebrews 2:14-15, when was this accomplished? _____
_____
_____
_____

Does the Physical Nation of Israel Still Play a Role in God's Final Plans?

Some in the religious world argue that the modern nation of Israel continues to serve a function in events that will lead to Christ's Second Coming. Stephen Russell addresses this question, summarizing the arguments advanced by advocates of this view, then demonstrating the fulfillment of God's land, nation, and seed promises.

1. Did premillennialism have many proponents within the early years of church history? _____
   When did it grow in prominence within the religious world?
   _____

2. Does the presence or absence of a religious doctrine in church history necessarily mean that it is unscriptural? _____
   Explain your answer: _____

3. Summarize Ryrie's two issues that make the role of the nation of Israel a core premise of premillennial doctrine.
   1. _____
   _____
   2. _____
   _____

4. According to the author of this essay, upon what notion must proponents of premillennialism stand regarding "every promise and prophecy made concerning Israel"? _____
   _____

5. Do you take the Bible "literally"? _____
   _____

Does the Physical Nation of Israel Still Play a Role in God's Final Plans?

Is every passage of Scripture intended to be taken literally? Answer this question for the following Scriptures.

Matthew 5:29-30: _____
_____

Luke 14:26: _____
_____

Genesis 37:5-10: _____
_____

6. In the author's quote from John MacArthur, what verse from Matthew 24 does he not take literally? _____
   Why does MacArthur argue against taking it literally? _____
   _____

   What problems do you see with his argumentation? _____
   _____

7. In the essay, the author also quotes MacArthur regarding the Old Testament. Summarize his argument about the Old Testament.
   _____
   _____
   _____

   Ironically, advocates of the AD 70 Doctrine make a similar argument about the Old Testament but interpret all eschatological statements spiritually or figuratively. How can a proper attitude toward the New Testament help avoid both extremes? _____
   _____
   _____
   _____

Does the Physical Nation of Israel Still Play a Role in God's Final Plans?

8. What does Paul teach about Old Testament Scriptures in Colossians 1:25-27? _____

9. In 1 Peter 1:10-12, what does Peter say about those who penned Old Testament Scriptures? _____

10. Without the revelation of the gospel, would Jews living in Old Testament times have understood the point Paul made about Jesus as the "Rock" in 1 Corinthians 10:1-4? Why or why not? _____

11. Read the following Scriptures and note the promises made to Abraham and his descendants in each passage.
    Genesis 12:1-3: _____

    Genesis 13:16: _____

    Genesis 15:5, 18: _____

    Genesis 17:4-5: _____

    Genesis 26:5: _____

    Genesis 28:1-5: _____

12. What do premillennialists contend about the promises of Genesis 15:18? _____

13. In the quote the author offers in the essay, how does Walvoord explain that Christ has been a blessing to all nations? _____

    Does he view this as a physical or spiritual fulfillment? _____

Does the Physical Nation of Israel Still Play a Role in God's Final Plans?

14. What time marker is given with the land promise in Genesis 15:13-16? _____

15. What does Exodus 3:6 indicate about the time and circumstances in which the land promise would be fulfilled? _____

16. What does Joshua 21:43 claim about when God fulfilled His land promise to Abraham? _____

    What must premillennialists argue about the meaning of this passage? _____

    Do you see any problems with their argument? _____

17. In the author's quote in the essay, summarize the point MacArthur makes about the connection between premillennialism and Calvinism (i.e. "sovereign grace and election"). _____

18. What conditions does God set in Deuteronomy 30:15-20? _____

19. How are these conditions restated in Joshua 23:14-16? _____

20. How do the words of Jesus in Matthew 23:37-38 reflect the presence of conditions which God expected the Jews to meet? _____

Does the Physical Nation of Israel Still Play a Role in God's Final Plans?

21. If God set no conditions for covenantal or salvation promises who would be to blame for condemnation? _____

22. In Genesis 49:10, how is the seed promise "bestowed exclusively" to Judah? _____

23. According to 2 Samuel 7:12-13, through whom would the seed promise later be bestowed? _____

24. To whom is the language of 2 Samuel 7 applied in 1 Kings 8:19-20? _____

25. What does Solomon say about all the promise God made through Moses in 1 Kings 8:56? _____

26. Summarize the author's argument explaining how Paul's application of Jesus as fulfillment of the "Seed" promise in Galatians 3:16 is not a contradiction of 2 Samuel 7:12-13. _____

27. From the author's quote of Lindsey, what do premillennialists argue regarding the Law of Moses? _____

28. Explain the author's point that it offers a more "complete picture" to say that the New Testament has "fulfilled" rather "replaced" the Old Testament. _____

29. Explain how the author relates the following passages to Christ's fulfillment of laws set forth in the book of Leviticus.
    Hebrews 10:10: _____

    Hebrews 7:26-28 and Revelation 1:6: _____

Does the Physical Nation of Israel Still Play a Role in God's Final Plans?

Galatians 3:24-25: _____

Romans 13:9-10: _____

30. In John 5:45-46, what did Jesus tell the Jews they would do if they truly listened to Moses? _____

31. List some identifiers Paul offers in Philippians 3:4-5 to demonstrate his connection to fleshly Israel. _____

32. What does Paul declare about Christians in Galatians 3:29? _____

33. Explain Paul's point about the children of Hagar and Sarai in Galatians 4:21-31. _____

    What bearing might this have on the questions considered in this essay? _____

34. What does Paul assert in Romans 9:6? _____

    What bearing might this have on the questions considered in this essay? _____

35. One of the identifiers noted above of Jewish citizenship was circumcision of the flesh. According to Romans 2:28-29 does circumcision of the flesh identify one as a citizen of spiritual Israel? _____

Does the Physical Nation of Israel Still Play a Role in God's Final Plans?

What bearing might this have on the questions considered in this essay? _____
_____

36. What does Paul say about this spiritual circumcision in Philippians 3:3? _____
_____

One final time, what bearing might this have on the questions considered in this essay? _____
_____

37. What does the author quote Piper to say about the concept that the physical promises to Israel have now been made spiritual? _____
_____
_____

What does MacArthur call this interpretation? _____
_____

38. What is Zerubbabel asked in Zechariah 4:10? _____
_____
_____

How might we do the same thing? _____
_____
_____

39. Does it weaken a promise of God to say that it has a spiritual fulfillment? Why or why not? _____
_____

Does it dishonor the Lord's church to consider it an afterthought or a "placeholder" because the Jews rejected Christ? Why or why not?
_____
_____
_____

Does the Physical Nation of Israel Still Play a Role in God's Final Plans?

40. In Hebrews 8:5, which things represented the "copy" and "shadow" and which represented the "true"? _____
_____
_____

41. Explain the author's summary of the book of Romans in each of the following sections.
Romans 1-3: _____
_____

Romans 4-6: _____
_____

Romans 7-8: _____
_____

Romans 9-11: _____
_____

42. In Romans 11:2-4, Paul cites an incident recorded in 1 Kings 18:9-18. What is the incident and how is Paul using this incident in his argument in Romans? _____
_____
_____
_____

43. Explain the agricultural illustration Paul uses in Romans 11:15-23.
_____
_____
_____

According to this illustration, what would allow fleshly Israel to be "grafted in" again? _____
_____

"When Will These Things Be?" : Questions on Eschatology

44. In light of the context and teaching that precedes it, explain Romans 11:26a, "all Israel will be saved." _____
   _____
   _____
   _____

   Is this referring to fleshly Israel or spiritual Israel? Why or why not?
   _____
   _____
   _____

   What bearing does this have on the questions considered in this essay? _____
   _____
   _____
   _____

Can Signs Foretell When the End Will Come?

The final essay in this section was written by Allen Dvorak and considers signs and what they tell us about when the end will come. Documenting various failed attempts to interpret events and predict the end, the study looks at five key Scriptures that inform us about the end, what will happen, and whether or not signs can indicate its coming.

1. How does 2 Peter 3:10 prove the world will end? _____
   _____
   _____

2. When did David Montaigne predict the end would come? _____

3. What premise leads to the conclusion that large scale catastrophes can indicate that Christ is coming or the world is about to end?
   _____
   _____

4. What does the scientific theory that our sun will one day become a "red giant" presume to foretell? _____
   _____

   When do theorists predict this will happen? _____

5. When did William Miller predict Christ would return?_____
   _____

   With what religious group was Miller associated? _____
   _____

"When Will These Things Be?": Questions on Eschatology

6. In what two ways did his followers react to this failed prediction? _____
   _____

7. Who became associated with the second group of Miller's followers? _____
   What religious group grew out of this? _____
   _____

8. When did Russel and N. H. Barbour, say an "invisible coming" of the Lord took place? _____
   What did they call the 40-year period after this? _____

9. List some things from the quotes of Russel's writings that he predicted would happen in association with the close of this 40-year period:
   _____
   _____
   _____
   _____

10. List some things from the quotes of Russel's writings that he predicted would characterize the millennial kingdom he claimed would begin at this time: _____
    _____
    _____
    _____
    _____

    Do such conditions now exist? _____

11. How is this failed prediction explained away in the Publishers' Foreword to Volume 2 of *Studies in the Scriptures*? _____
    _____
    _____

12. Explain the pattern that Jehovah's Witnesses followed in offering two approaches to dealing with false predictions:
    1. _____
    2. _____

Can Signs Foretell When the End Will Come?

Read Deuteronomy 18:20-22. How did this text teach the Israelites to interpret failed predictions from prophets? _____
_____

13. How do atheists view the willingness of "religious people" to rationalize away failed predictions? _____
_____

14. Summarize what each of these passages indicate about God's knowledge of the future.
    Isaiah 46:8-10: _____
    _____

    Isaiah 44:6-8: _____
    _____

    Isaiah 48:3-5: _____
    _____

15. What did Jesus tell His disciples they could look for as a sign that the destruction of Jerusalem was about to happen (Matt. 24:15-16; Luke 21:20-21)? _____
    _____

16. Why do many look to the book of Revelation to find signs pointing to when Jesus will return? _____
    _____

17. What type of literature is the book of Revelation? _____

    How does the author of this essay define this type of literature? _____
    _____

    How can it be said to "cover" and "uncover" its message? _____
    _____
    _____

"When Will These Things Be?" : Questions on Eschatology

18. What are some figures used in Revelation 13 and 17? _____
_____
_____

19. What are some interpretations that people have made of the great prostitute described in Revelation? _____
_____
_____

20. In this essay, the author uses Micah 1:3 and Matthew 16:28 as examples of "comings" of the Lord that are not the final Second Coming of Jesus. Look at the context of each passage and explain from it what supports this conclusion.
    Micah 1:3: _____
    _____
    _____

    Matthew 16:28: _____
    _____
    _____

21. In the essay, the author uses 2 Peter 3:1-10 and Hebrews 9:28 in support of his statement "it is clear from Scripture that Christ will 'come' again at the end of time." Look at the context of each passage and explain from it what supports this conclusion.
    2 Peter 3:1-10: _____
    _____
    _____

    Hebrews 9:28: _____
    _____
    _____

22. What two factors determine which "coming" is addressed?
    1. _____
    2. _____

23. According to Revelation 20:11-15, in relation to judgment of all souls before God, when will death be destroyed? _____
_____
_____

Can Signs Foretell When the End Will Come?

24. According to 1 Corinthians 15:21-26, what are some things that take place in association with the destruction of death? _____
_____
_____

25. What does Revelation 20:1-10 teach about Satan during the 1,000-year period of Christ's reign? _____
_____
_____

26. Look at the following Scriptures the author offers to demonstrate the use of the term "thousand" to indicate "a large, but not exact quantity." What do you see in the texts that supports his conclusion?
Psalm 50:10: _____

Psalm 84:1-10: _____

2 Peter 3:8: _____

If the Holy Spirit does the same thing in Revelation 20:3-4, what might that indicate about how to interpret this?_____
_____
_____

27. The author asserts that a "basic principle for the interpretation o biblical passages is to interpret the 'hard' passages in light of the 'easy' passages." Explain the rationale behind this principle. Do you believe this principle is sound? Can you think of a Scripture which demonstrates its validity? _____
_____
_____
_____
_____

"When Will These Things Be?" : Questions on Eschatology

28. If Scripture teaches that Jesus will return "as a thief in the night" (1 Thess. 5:1-3; 2 Pet. 3:10), how would it be a contradiction of this teaching if the book of Revelation offered signs indicating exactly when it would occur? _____
_____

29. In his essay, what statement of Jesus in Matthew 23:38 does the author suggest may have motivated the disciples' question about the temple in Matthew 24:1? _____
_____

30. What did Jesus say about the temple in Matthew 24:2? _____
_____

31. What verse in Matthew 24 does the author suggest some see as the "transition verse" moving away from discussing the destruction of the temple to teachings regarding the final coming of Jesus and the end of the world? _____
    What do you see in this verse that could lead some to make this argument? _____
    _____
    _____

32. What type of language (which we discussed earlier regarding the book of Revelation) does the author identify in Matthew 24:29? _____
    _____

    Based on Isaiah 13:1, 9-10, 13, what does the author argue we "cannot conclude" without "contextual evidence"? _____
    _____
    _____

    What type of judgment is described in Isaiah 13? _____
    _____

Can Signs Foretell When the End Will Come?

33. What verse in Matthew 24 does the author suggest acts as a "chronological marker" for the fulfillment of the things Jesus predicted? _____

    What do you see in this verse that supports this argument? _____
    _____

34. If Matthew 24:34 and 36 demonstrate a transition to teaching about the final coming of Jesus, does the Lord offer any signs to indicate when it would happen? _____
    _____

35. What had some in Thessalonica misunderstood about Christ's coming that led him to clarify it in his first epistle? _____
    _____

36. What does 1 Thessalonians 5:2 indicate about the timing of when Christ will return? _____
    _____

    What does this indicate about how to answer the question posed in the title of this essay? _____
    _____

    Does Paul point to any signs in 1 Thessalonians 4 and 5 that could be signs to indicate when the end will occur? _____

37. Earlier in the essay the author noted some who have argued that the Lord came silently on some occasion they identify. How does 1 Thessalonians 4:16 refute these claims? _____
    _____
    _____

38. According to 1 Thessalonians 5:4-8, what benefit comes from being prepared for the Lord's coming, whenever it may be? _____
    _____
    _____
    _____

"When Will These Things Be?" : Questions on Eschatology

39. According to 2 Thessalonians 2:3, what would happen before the Lord's final coming? _____
   _____

   From the context, are the descriptions of these things so specific that they constitute signs that can be observed to predict the exact time of Christ's return? Why or why not? _____
   _____

40. In a footnote within this essay, how does the author say some have identified the "man of lawlessness" of 2 Thessalonians 2:3 and what theory is asserted with this identification? _____
   _____
   _____
   _____

   What two observations does the author make about the biblical use of this term?
   1. _____
      _____
   2. _____
      _____

41. List some things Jesus indicates about the timing of His coming in Luke 12:35-40. _____
   _____
   _____

   If this describes His final coming, does it promise signs that will indicate its imminence? _____
   What does He urge His disciples to do? _____
   _____

42. What three possibilities does the author offer as identifications of the "Day" mentioned in Hebrews 10:25?
   1. _____
   2. _____
   3. _____
   Some have argued for a fourth possibility as well. What do you think it might be? _____

Can Signs Foretell When the End Will Come?

43. What interpretation does the author of this essay find to be the most likely? _____
    Explain what leads him to this conclusion? _____
    _____
    _____

    Why does he reject the other two possibilities? _____
    _____
    _____

    Do you agree with his conclusions? Why or why not? ____
    _____
    _____

44. If the "Day" in Hebrews 10:25 refers to the final coming of Jesus, does the text indicate it may be predicted by signs? _____

45. What question do scoffers ask in 2 Peter 3:4? _____
    _____

    Do scoffers ask this question today? If so, why? _____
    _____

46. What does Peter's statement in 2 Peter 3:10 about when Jesus will return indicate about how to answer the question posed in the title of this essay? _____
    _____
    _____

    Does Peter point to any signs that may be observed to indicate it is about to happen? _____

47. What is the definition of "progressive revelation"? _____
    _____

48. If someone claimed to receive direct revelation from God that the end would come at a certain time and it did not, what must we conclude about such a person? _____
    _____

"When Will These Things Be?" : Questions on Eschatology

49. Based on the wording of Deuteronomy 29:29 and Matthew 24:36, can we conclude that the exact time of Jesus's return is a "secret thing"? Why or why not? _____
_____
_____

50. What did Peter urge his readers to do in light of the certainty of Christ's Second Coming (2 Pet. 3:11, 14)? _____
_____
_____

Judgment Day

What Does the Bible Teach about the Coming of Christ?
　Kevin Kay

What Is the Biblical Teaching on the Resurrection?
　Bruce Reeves

Does the Bible Teach the "Rapture," the Coming of an Antichrist, and the Battle of Armageddon?
　Mark Mayberry

"When Will These Things Be?"
Questions on Eschatology

What Does the Bible Teach about the Coming of Christ?

The first essay on Judgment Day was written by Kevin Kay and focuses on the coming of Jesus. After examining ten things the Bible teaches that the coming will (or should) be, the essay considers how biblical teaching refutes common error taught on the subject.

1. Read Hebrews 9:26-28 and answer the following questions.
   To what does the phrase "He has appeared" refer in 9:26? _____
   _____

   To what does the phrase "He will appear" refer in 9:28?_____
   _____

   Does this infer anything about the nature of these appearances?
   _____
   _____

   Does this wording allow for an unseen appearance? Why or why not?_____
   _____

   Explain the phrase "apart from sin," and address whether this has yet been fulfilled. _____
   _____
   _____
   _____

2. In John 14:1-3, explain the phrase "that where I am, there you may be also" and address whether it has yet been fulfilled. _____
   _____
   _____
   _____

"When Will These Things Be?" : Questions on Eschatology

3. Identify the following parables that allude to the Second Coming of Jesus from the Scriptures listed and what each says about it?
   Matthew 13:24-30; 36-43:_____
   _____

   Matthew 13:47-50: _____
   _____

   Matthew 25:1, 5-6, 10, 13:_____
   _____

   Matthew 25:14-15, 19, 27:_____
   _____

   Luke 12:35-48: _____
   _____

   Luke 19:12-13, 15, 23:_____
   _____

4. What did angels promise the disciples in Acts 1:9-11?_____
   _____
   _____

5. Read the following Scriptures the author classifies as brief references to the Lord's Second Coming and summarize what each teaches about it.
   Peter (Acts 13:19-20; 1 Pet. 1:7, 13; 5:4):_____
   _____

   Paul (1 Cor. 1:7-8; 4:5; 11:26; Col. 3:4; 1 Tim. 6:14; 2 Tim. 4:1, 8; Titus 2:13):_____
   _____
   _____
   _____

   Writer of Hebrews (Heb. 9:27-28): _____
   _____

   John (1 John 2:28; 3:2):_____
   _____
   _____

What Does the Bible Teach about the Coming of Christ?

Jude (Jude 14-15): _____
_____

6. From the lists the author provides of the biblical use of four key terms applied to the coming of Jesus, list some of the examples that demonstrate the scope of the use of each term with scriptural citations.
   "Coming" (or "Presence"): _____
   _____
   _____
   _____

   "Revelation": _____
   _____
   _____
   _____

   "Appearing" (or "Brightness"): _____
   _____
   _____
   _____

   "Appearance": _____
   _____
   _____

7. From a footnote in the essay, how does Vine define the Greek word *parousia*? _____
   _____
   _____

8. From a footnote in the essay, summarize the author's quote from Ladd regarding the force of the word *apokalupsis* as applied to the Second Coming of Jesus. _____
   _____
   _____
   _____
   _____

"When Will These Things Be?" : Questions on Eschatology

9. From the author's lists of different ways the day of the Lord's coming is described, list some examples the author provides with Scriptures.

   A Day of Manifestation: _____
   _____
   _____

   A Day of Visitation: _____
   _____
   _____

   A Day of Significance: _____
   _____
   _____

10. What three basic concepts does the author suggest are involved in the Old Testament use of the term "day of the Lord" in the sense of a "day of reckoning"?
    1. _____
    2. _____
    3. _____

11. From the list the author offers of days of reckoning for various nations list a few you find the most compelling and summarize what the Scriptures say about them. _____
    _____
    _____
    _____
    _____
    _____

12. List ten thing the author suggests the Second Coming of Christ will be (or should be).
    1. _____
    2. _____
    3. _____

What Does the Bible Teach about the Coming of Christ?

   4. _____
   5. _____
   6. _____
   7. _____
   8. _____
   9. _____
   10. _____
13. How did Jesus come and preach peace to those who "were afar off" as described in Ephesians 2:17 (cf. John 14:16-18; Matt. 15:24)? _____
   _____
   _____

14. From one of the footnotes to his essay, list the ten comings of the Lord the author offers with Scriptures that describe them.

   1. _____
   2. _____
   3. _____
   4. _____
   5. _____
   6. _____
   7. _____
   8. _____
   9. _____
   10. _____

"When Will These Things Be?": Questions on Eschatology

15. Advocates of the AD 70 Doctrine mock the idea that Scripture speaks of multiple "comings" of the Lord, seeking to apply virtually all post-incarnation comings to AD 70. From the list offered in the previous question, what are some consequences that would result if their argument was true? _____
_____
_____

16. Read Matthew 16:27, Mark 8:38, and Luke 9:26 and make note of what these texts teach about Christ's return. _____
_____
_____

17. Until what does Acts 3:19-20 teach the "heavens must receive" Jesus? _____
_____

    What are some things this infers about Christ's return? _____

18. In Philippians 3:20-21, what did Paul teach would happen to the saved when Jesus comes? _____

19. Explain the significance of Paul saying that "the Lord Himself will descend from heaven" (1 Thess. 4:16). Does this allow for a figurative or representative coming? Why or why not? _____
_____
_____

20. According to Colossians 3:4 when does Paul teach that the saved with "appear with Him in glory"? _____

    How do the following passages reflect the same idea?
    1 Timothy 6:14-15: _____

What Does the Bible Teach about the Coming of Christ?

1 John 2:28: _____

21. What is the definition of the word *phaneroō*, translated "appears" in Colossians 3:4? _____

22. What does John say about who will see Jesus when He returns (Rev. 1:7)? _____

    How does this wording compare to Matthew 24:30? _____

23. List three things that will be heard when Jesus returns (1 Thess. 4:16).
    1. _____ 2. _____
    3. _____

24. Read the following Scriptures and make note of what each says about when Jesus will return.
    Matthew 24:36: _____

    Matthew 24:42: _____

    Matthew 24:44: _____

    Matthew 25:13: _____

    Mark 13:32-33: _____

    Mark 13:35: _____

    Given the emphasis within these texts should we believe that anyone can predict the time of the Lord's return? _____

25. In Matthew 24:37-39, to what does Jesus compare the unexpected nature of the time of His Second Coming? _____

"When Will These Things Be?" : Questions on Eschatology

How does Paul echo this same idea (1 Thess. 5:3)? _____
_____

26. Some have argued that although Jesus taught that the time of His Second Coming was unknown while He was on earth (Matt. 24:36), the promise of further revelation through the Holy Spirit (John 16:13) allowed New Testament writers to know and claim it was "at hand" (Jas. 5: 8) or coming "quickly" (Rev. 22:20). If this argument is true, why would both Paul and Peter echo the Lord's words that He would come as a thief (1 Thess. 5:1-2; 2 Pet. 3:10, cf. Matt. 24:43)? _____
_____
_____
_____
_____

27. List the names of those associated with the following dates of failed predictions of Christ's return:
    1843: _____
    March 21, 1844: _____
    October 22, 1844: _____
    1914: _____
    1918: _____
    1925: _____
    1975: _____
    June 28, 1981: _____
    September 13, 1988: _____
    1988: _____
    1989: _____

28. Read Luke 12:40-44 and 2 Peter 3:9 and answer the following questions.
    Can man do anything to prevent or delay the Lord's return? _____
    _____
    Will our failure to be prepared delay His coming? _____
    _____

What Does the Bible Teach about the Coming of Christ?

Why has the Lord delayed? _____
_____

29. How do Matthew 25:31-32 and Acts 17:30-31 demonstrate that the Second Coming of Jesus is inescapable? _____
_____
_____
_____

30. When does 2 Timothy 4:1 say the living and dead will be judged?
_____

    Since Christ's kingdom was established on Pentecost, how may we understand reference to "coming and His kingdom" in this passage?
_____
_____

31. What is eschatology? _____
    How does 1 Corinthians 15:20-24 demonstrate that Paul is discussing eschatology? _____
_____

32. List the fifteen events the author outlines as a chronology of the last day and offer some of the Scriptures which demonstrate his arrangement.

    1. _____
    _____
    2. _____
    _____
    3. _____
    _____
    4. _____
    _____
    5. _____
    _____
    6. _____
    _____
    7. _____
    _____

"When Will These Things Be?" : Questions on Eschatology

8. _____

8. _____

9. _____

10. _____

11. _____

12. _____

13. _____

14. _____

15. _____

33. Explain the syllogism the author frames regarding the resurrection of the righteous and the unrighteous. _____

34. When Paul taught the Athenians, whom did he say would act as Judge of all (Acts 17:30-31)? _____
What did he say God has "appointed"? _____

35. According to John 12:48 what will be the standard by which souls will be judged? _____

What Does the Bible Teach about the Coming of Christ?

36. What are some of the things the author lists will be judged on that day? Provide Scriptures. _____
   _____
   _____
   _____
   _____

37. Explain what the author means by describing the Second Coming as "potential." _____
   _____
   _____
   _____
   _____

38. After discussing the events that will occur when Jesus returns, Peter asks his reader's the question "what manner of persons ought you to be. . . ?" (2 Pet. 3:11). List the ten adjectives the author offers in answer to this question.
   1. _____   2. _____
   3. _____   4. _____
   5. _____   6. _____
   7. _____   8. _____
   9. _____ 10. _____

39. For what does Titus 2:13 teach that Christians should be looking? _____
   _____

40. According to 1 Thessalonians 4:13-18, what can Christians have that others do not have when they grieve? _____

41. In 1 Peter 4:12-14, what does Peter say the Christian may have when the glory of Christ is revealed? _____
   _____

42. What does James urge his readers to be "until the coming of the Lord" (Jas. 5:7-11)? _____
   To what vocation does he compare this? Explain his point. _____
   _____
   _____

"When Will These Things Be?" : Questions on Eschatology

43. What does the writer of Hebrews tell his readers they need (Heb. 10:36-39)? _____

44. How does Peter teach Christians to conduct themselves (1 Pet. 1:17-19)? _____
    How did Paul describe this (2 Cor. 5:10-11)? _____
    _____

45. List the attributes Peter encourages Christians to have in the following passages.
    1 Peter 1:13-16: _____
    _____

    2 Peter 3:10-14: _____
    _____

46. In the Parable of the Expectant Steward, who does Jesus describe as "blessed" (Luke 12:35-44)? _____
    _____
    _____

47. List the conditions specified in the following Scriptures under which one will be blessed in the Judgment.
    Colossians 1:21-23: _____
    _____

    Hebrews 3:6, 14: _____
    _____

    Revelation 2:10: _____
    _____

48. Summarize what the following three religious systems teach about the Second Coming of Jesus.
    Jehovah's Witnesses: _____
    _____
    _____

    Dispensationalists: _____
    _____
    _____
    _____

What Does the Bible Teach about the Coming of Christ?

Realized eschatologists: _____
_____
_____
_____

49. From a footnote in the essay, explain how dispensationalists are divided over the sequence of Christ's coming. _____
_____
_____
_____

50. From a footnote, list the various names by which realized eschatology is known. _____
_____
_____

51. Explain the author's argument that an invisible coming of Jesus in 1914, as Jehovah's Witnesses claim, is refuted by the teaching of the New Testament. _____
_____
_____

52. How does Hebrews 9:28 refute the theory that Jesus will come in stages, as dispensationalism teaches? _____
_____
_____
_____

53. To refute the dispensational teaching that different terms can apply to different stages of Christ's coming, the author offers several examples of times when various terms are used interchangeably. Using the examples the author cites, answer the following questions.

97

"When Will These Things Be?" : Questions on Eschatology

To what event did Jesus apply the words *parousia* ("presence") and *erchomai* ("coming") interchangeably (Matt. 24:37-44)? _____
_____

To what event did Paul apply the words *apocalypsis* ("revelation"), *erchomai* ("coming"), *parousia* ("presence"), and *epiphaneia* ("appearing") interchangeably (2 Thess. 1:6-10; 2:1-2, 8)? _____
_____

To what event did John apply the words *parousia* ("presence"), and *epiphaneia* ("appear") in 1 John 2:28-3:2? _____
_____
_____

54. Using the chart from the essay, fill-in the empty blanks below:

Dispensationalism vs. The New Testament	
The "Rapture"	**The Resurrection**
Invisible Coming	
	Public Coming (1 Thess. 4:16)
	Christ Comes *for* (1 Thess. 4:14) and *with* His Saints to God (1 Thess. 3:13)
Righteous Dead Raised before *Unrighteous* Dead	
Righteous Raised *1,007* Years before the Last Day	
Wicked Left Behind	
	Righteous Rewarded (1 Thess. 4:15-18) and *Wicked* Punished (2 Thess. 1:6-10)
Marriage Supper In Heaven for Saints and Tribulation on Earth for Wicked	
	Second Coming (Heb. 9:26-28)
	One Resurrection: Righteous and Wicked (John 5:28-29)

What Does the Bible Teach about the Coming of Christ?

55. Dispensationalism teaches that there will be two resurrections separated by 1,007 years. How do 1 Corinthians 15:20-24 and John 5:28-29 indicate that all the dead will be raised together at "the end"?
_____
_____
_____

56. What does Matthew 10:23 say about the coming of the Lord? _____
_____
_____

    To what coming does this refer? Explain your answer. _____
    _____
    _____

57. In Matthew 16:27 and 28 note what is said about comings of Jesus.
_____
_____
_____

    Is "coming in His kingdom" (v. 28) the same as when He "will come in the glory of His Father" to "reward each according to his works" (v. 27)? Why or why not? _____
    _____
    _____

    Which coming did Jesus say some would see before they would "taste death"? _____

58. Advocates of realized eschatology build many of their arguments upon the assertion that the Greek word *mellō*, translated "shall" in Matthew 16:27, always means "is about to" (i.e. "the Son f Man *is about to* come"). Look at the following texts the author offers where *mellō* is used and identify the time gap described.
    Matthew 11:14 (cf. Mal. 4:5-6): _____
    _____
    _____

    Acts 26:22-23 (cf. Deut. 18:18): _____
    _____
    _____

"When Will These Things Be?" : Questions on Eschatology

Romans 5:14: _____
_____

Galatians 3:23: _____
_____

Colossians 2:16-17: _____
_____

Hebrews 10:1: _____
_____

If these things allow for long time intervals can one insist that Matthew 10:27 must be a short time interval? _____
_____

59. If Judgment Day would occur in AD 70 when Jerusalem was destroyed by Rome, why would Felix, a Roman governor, be terrified by a discussion with Paul about the "judgment to come" (Acts 24:24-25)? _____
_____
_____

60. What imminent comings of the Lord were promised in the following passages?
John 14:16-18, 28: _____
_____

Acts 1:4-5: _____
_____

Do all imminent comings point to AD 70? _____

61. What do the following passages teach about a delay in the departure and return of the one being described?
Matthew 24:48-51: _____
_____

Matthew 25:5: _____
_____

Matthew 25:19: _____
_____

2 Thessalonians 2:1-5: _____
_____

What Does the Bible Teach about the Coming of Christ?

2 Peter 3:4: _____
_____

Does this infer that there may be a delay in the Lord's return? Why or why not? _____
_____

62. Read Acts 1:9-11 and note all that the text says about the "manner" in which Christ ascended. _____
_____

What does this indicate if He is promised to return "in like manner"? _____
_____

Did any of this happen in AD 70? _____

63. Explain the author's syllogism about the Lord returning bodily and visibly. _____
_____

64. Explain the author's quote "When the plain sense makes good sense, any other sense is nonsense." Do you agree with this statement? How does it apply to the teachings of realized eschatology? _____
_____
_____
_____

65. What relationship does Paul teach exists between the observance of the Lord's Supper and Christ's coming (1 Cor. 11:23-26)? _____
_____

If Christ came in AD 70 why continue to observe the Lord's Supper?
_____
_____
_____

"When Will These Things Be?" : Questions on Eschatology

66. List four beliefs the author attests that are clearly demonstrated in early writings by Christians immediately after the New Testament and the sources they can be found.

   1. _____

   2. _____

   3. _____

   4. _____

What Is the Biblical Teaching on the Resurrection?

The New Testament clearly associates the resurrection with the events of Judgment Day, but what is the nature of this resurrection? Will it be a bodily resurrection or is it purely spiritual? Has it already occurred and what relationship does it have to the resurrection of Jesus? Bruce Reeves explores this question in the second essay on Judgment Day.

1. In Job 14:14, what question did Job ask that still troubles the human mind today? _____
_____

2. Explain how Jesus connects the wording of Exodus 3:6 with the resurrection in Matthew 22:29-32. _____
_____
_____
_____
_____

3. Why do you think some consider the concept of a bodily resurrection "unreasonable and unbelievable"? _____
_____

4. What is said about the false teaching of Hymenaeus and Philetus (2 Tim. 2:16-18)? _____
_____

What does this tell us about modern doctrines that advocate the same concepts? _____
_____

"When Will These Things Be?" : Questions on Eschatology

5. Explain the three examples of figurative references to resurrection cited by the author in the following passages and how it can be demonstrated that each is figurative.
   Ezekiel 37:1-14: _____
   _____

   Revelation 6:9-11; 20:5-6: _____
   _____

   Romans 6:4-6: _____
   _____

6. In scriptural examples of the dead being raised (such as 1 Kings 17:17-24; 2 Kings 4:32-37; 13:20-21; Matt. 27:52-53; Mark 5:35-43; Luke 7:11-17; John 11:39-44; Acts 9:40; 20:9-10), why does the author suggest these are best understood as "miraculous resuscitations"?
   _____
   _____

   How does the resurrection of Jesus differ from these? _____
   _____

7. The author asserts that concepts such as *resurrection, coming,* and *judgment* are "grounded in the literal reality of such concepts." Can you think of other examples in Scripture where this is clearly demonstrated? _____
   _____

   Can you think of any example of a figurative concept that is not grounded in some literal reality? If so, what is it? _____
   _____

8. In the author's quote from Dan King, what does King claim is a "given in Old Testament research"? _____
   _____

9. What do some claim about the Old Testament and resurrection?
   _____

What Is the Biblical Teaching on the Resurrection?

If this was true, how can we explain the conflict that existed between the Pharisees and Sadducees over resurrection (see Acts 23:8)? _____
_____

10. We explored above Jesus's application of Exodus 3:6 to the question posed by the Sadducees in Matthew 22:29-32. Considering Luke's account, what did the Sadducees ask (see Luke 20:27-38)? _____
_____

11. What does Jesus say about "this age" in contrast to "the age to come" (Luke 20:34-35)? _____
_____

    With which age does Jesus associate the resurrection? _____
_____

12. How do advocates of realized eschatology attempt to explain this passage? _____

    Do you see problems with their explanation? If so, what are they?
_____
_____

13. Some argue that by saying "all live to Him" (Luke 20:38) Jesus was saying Abraham, Isaac, and Jacob were already in a resurrected state (defining resurrection as purely spiritual rather than bodily). How does the author refute this argument? _____
_____
_____

14. Read Hosea 13:14 and 1 Corinthians 15:56-57 and explain Paul's use of this passage in the context of 1 Corinthians. _____
_____
_____

"When Will These Things Be?" : Questions on Eschatology

15. Read Psalm 16:10 and Acts 2:25-31 and explain Peter's use of this text in application to the resurrection of Jesus. _____
   _____
   _____

16. To what historical event does Daniel 10 and 11 point? _____
   _____
   _____

Full-preterists argue that Daniel 12:1-3 points to a spiritual resurrection that happened in the destruction of Jerusalem in AD 70 rather than a post-death vindication of the faithful that is promised in a final worldwide judgment at the end of time. Read the text before and after this and identify problems the text poses to this theory.
   _____
   _____
   _____

17. In the author's quote from Goldingay, summarize his explanation of the force of Daniel 12:1-3. _____
   _____
   _____

18. What similarities are there between Daniel 12:1-3 and the words of Jesus in John 5:28-29? _____
   _____
   _____

19. Full-preterists argue that "holy people" in Daniel 12:7 is used of Israel as a whole, and then try to identify the "shattering" of the "holy people" with the destruction of Jerusalem in AD 70. In the context, to whom does the phrase "holy people" refer in Daniel 8:23-24? _____
   _____
   _____

What Is the Biblical Teaching on the Resurrection?

20. Read Daniel 11:31, 12:11, and Matthew 24:15. In Jesus's use of the phrase "abomination of desolation," is He using it of the same event prophesied in Daniel or another event that would be like it? _____
   _____
   _____
   _____

21. In the author's quote from Lenski, summarize his explanation of Jesus's use of the phrase "abomination of desolation" from Daniel.
   _____
   _____
   _____

22. What is Daniel told in Daniel 12:13? _____
   _____

23. In the author's quote from Pope about Daniel 12:13, explain his point from the use of the word "arise" and "the end of the days" in that text.
   _____
   _____
   _____

24. Where can the most extensive teaching on resurrection in the New Testament be found? _____
   What problem is Paul addressing in this text? _____
   _____
   _____
   _____

25. List some fundamental facts of the gospel declared in 1 Corinthians 15:1-4. _____
   _____
   _____
   _____

"When Will These Things Be?" : Questions on Eschatology

26. In 1 Corinthians 15, what does Paul fear that a rejection of a future bodily resurrection of the dead could eventually lead them to reject?
    _____
    _____

    From a footnote in his essay, how does the author demonstrate this very problem among modern-day advocates of realized eschatology?
    _____
    _____
    _____

27. Advocates of realized eschatology (or the AD 70 Doctrine) argue that some in Corinth were denying the figurative resurrection of a cause or the spiritual gathering to be accomplished in the destruction of Jerusalem. How could such a denial lead to a denial of the bodily resurrection of Jesus? _____
    _____
    _____
    _____

28. Explain Paul's question in 1 Corinthians 15:12. _____
    _____
    _____

29. List what Paul correlates in the following passages.
    1 Corinthians 15:12: _____
    1 Corinthians 15:13: _____
    1 Corinthians 15:15: _____
    1 Corinthians 15:16: _____
    1 Corinthians 15:18: _____

30. What false doctrine did Hymenaeus and Philetus teach (2 Tim. 2:16-18)? _____
    _____

    How did Paul characterize the spread of this teaching and its effect on others? _____
    _____

What Is the Biblical Teaching on the Resurrection?

31. List six areas of faith the author suggests that are impacted by accepting the AD 70 Doctrine.
    1. _____
    2. _____
    3. _____
    4. _____
    5. _____
    6. _____

32. In Acts 24:15, what did Paul affirm that he believed? _____

33. In John 11:24, what did Martha say would happen to her brother "on the last day"? _____

34. Explain Paul's reference to "first fruits" in 1 Corinthians 15:20 and 23. _____

    What does this infer about the nature of the resurrection of "those who are Christ's at His coming"? _____

35. In 1 Corinthians 15:21-22, is Paul discussing physical death or spiritual death? Explain your answer. _____

36. Explain the author's assertion that if spiritual death is the focus of 1 Corinthians 15:21-22, the phrase "all shall be made alive" makes universalism the logical consequence of this passage. _____

"When Will These Things Be?" : Questions on Eschatology

37. How did Adam's sin bring physical death to mankind (Gen. 3:17-19)? _____
   _____
   _____

   How "in Christ" will "all "be made alive"? _____
   _____
   _____

38. Explain what the Hebrew writer says about the effect the death of Jesus had on mankind (Heb. 2:9-18). _____
   _____
   _____

39. In what the author calls the "dictionary of the preterists," how must realized eschatologists redefine the following terms throughout 1 Corinthians 15?
   Death: _____
   Resurrection: _____
   Body: _____
   In this passage, what problems do you see with these redefinitions?
   _____
   _____
   _____
   _____

40. In Acts 17:32, what led some in his audience to mock Paul? _____
   _____

   What was the makeup of his audience (Acts 17:18-22)? _____
   _____
   _____

41. In Acts 23:6-10, who objected to Paul's teaching on the resurrection?
   _____

42. What must full-preterists argue about Paul's focus in 1 Corinthians 15 for their theories to stand? _____
   _____

What Is the Biblical Teaching on the Resurrection?

What do we know about the makeup of the church in Corinth (Acts 18:1-17; 1 Cor. 1:21-24; 12:1-2)? _____
_____

43. Read 1 Corinthians 15::6, 18, 20; cf. 12, 16, 21-22, 26, 29, 32, 35, and 51 and determine to what Paul refers in the context in speaking of those who are "asleep." _____
_____

44. Explain the force of Paul's statement in 1 Corinthians 15:32. _____
_____
_____
_____

45. According to 1 Corinthians 15:24-28, until what things take place must Christ reign? _____
_____

Did these things happen in AD 70? _____

46. According to 1 Corinthians 15:24, what will Christ deliver to God the Father at that time? _____
Did that happen in AD 70? _____

47. Read 1 Corinthians 15:33-34. Would Paul agree with the claim some make that eschatological teachings have no affect on our everyday lives? Why or why not? _____
_____
_____

48. What question does Paul address in 1 Corinthians 15:35? _____
_____

To what "body" is Paul referring? Explain your answer. _____
_____
_____

"When Will These Things Be?" : Questions on Eschatology

49. Explain Paul's appeal to agriculture in his response to the question in 1 Corinthians 15:36-37. _____
_____
_____

50. The author asserts that Paul is discussing the transformation that will take place when the resurrection happens. How do Paul's words in Philippians 3:20-21 describe this? Is that text discussing the same thing? _____
_____
_____

51. Read 1 Corinthians 15:38-44 and answer the following questions. What does this text tell us about the nature of the resurrection?
_____
_____
_____

    Can the argument of full-preterists that "body" always refers to the church work in this text? Explain your answer. _____
_____
_____

    Is a "spiritual body" the same thing as simply a spirit? Explain your answer. _____
_____
_____

    Does a belief in a bodily resurrection hope for a raising of the unchanged physical body? Explain your answer. _____
_____
_____
_____

What Is the Biblical Teaching on the Resurrection?

52. Summarize the author's quote from Gorman. _____
_____
_____

53. From the author's quotes of Neubauer, how do full-preterists explain the problem in Corinth which Paul addresses in 1 Corinthians 15?
_____
_____
_____

   What problems do you see with this interpretation of the text?
_____
_____

54. Citing Williams, list the four consequences the author provides that result if this perspective is accepted.
   1. _____
   2. _____
   3. _____
   4. _____

55. What does John say about the hope Christians can have upon the Lord's return (1 John 3:2)? _____
_____
_____

   What may this suggest about the nature of the resurrection body?
_____
_____

"When Will These Things Be?" : Questions on Eschatology

56. Summarize the author's explanation of the force of Paul's declaration that "flesh and blood cannot inherit the kingdom of God" (1 Cor. 15:50-51). _____
   _____
   _____
   _____

   Does a belief in a bodily resurrection violate this passage? Explain your answer. _____
   _____
   _____

57. What will happen to those physically alive when Christ returns (1 Cor. 15:51-52)? _____
   _____
   _____

   Did this happen in AD 70? _____
   _____
   _____

58. As the author asserts, advocates of realized eschatology "frequently argue that the use of the singular term 'body' in Scripture uniformly refers to the corporate body of Christ." Read 1 Corinthians 6:9-20 and answer the following questions.
   How could the reference to the "stomach" apply if the "body" in this passage is the church (6:13)?_____
   _____

   What is Paul saying that God will "raise" (6:14)? _____
   _____

   Were the Corinthians already spiritual raised with Christ (6:9-11)?
   _____
   _____

   How could this be describing the church collectively if Paul speaks of "bodies" (plural) that are "members of Christ" (6:15-16)—doesn't the figure of the church as the "body" refer to the "body of Christ" (cf. 1 Cor. 12:27)?_____
   _____

What Is the Biblical Teaching on the Resurrection?

If Paul is discussing spiritual fornication would it not be sin against Christ's body rather than against one's "own body" (6:17-18)? _____

Doesn't this prove that Paul is describing sexual sin committed by one's own physical body? _____

In 1 Corinthians 6:10, the majority of manuscripts read "For you were bought at a price; therefore glorify God in your body and in your spirit, which are God's" (NKJV). If this is the true reading how could Paul be using "body" of the church? _____

59. In 2 Corinthians 4:1-14, how does Paul claim that the hope of resurrection allowed him to make it through the trials of life?
_____
_____

60. What three resurrections does the author point out in Romans 8:11?
    1. _____
    2. _____
    3. _____
    From the author's quote from Neubauer, how does he explain this passage? _____
    _____

    What two conclusions does the author assert that this view would force us to draw?
    1. _____

    2. _____

    Does the New Testament ever speak of the church as "mortal"?
    _____
    _____

115

"When Will These Things Be?" : Questions on Eschatology

Does the New Testament ever describe the church as "our body"? _____

61. What does Paul mean by the term "naked" in 2 Corinthians 5:1-3? _____
_____

Would not a rejection of a personal individual bodily resurrection be hoping to be "found naked"? Explain your answer. _____
_____
_____

62. From the author's quote from King, how did he explain the phrases "earthly tent" and "at home in the body" in 2 Corinthians 5:1-4?
_____
_____
_____

What problems do you see with this interpretation? _____
_____
_____

63. List the phrases the author notes in the following passages and show how they indicate that Paul is discussing the physical human body.
2 Corinthians 4:7: _____

2 Corinthians 4:10: _____

2 Corinthians 4:11: _____

2 Corinthians 4:16: _____

2 Corinthians 5:1: _____

2 Corinthians 5:2: _____

What Is the Biblical Teaching on the Resurrection?

2 Corinthians 5:4: _____
_____

64. What three factors does the author point out that demonstrate that there was a Gentile element within the church in Thessalonica when Paul wrote to them?

    1. _____
       _____

    2. _____
       _____

    3. _____
       _____

65. How far was Jerusalem away from Thessalonica? _____
    Would the destruction of Jerusalem bring deliverance and comfort to Christians in Thessalonica? Why or why not? _____
    _____
    _____

66. Read 1 Thessalonians 5:23. If Jesus came in the destruction f Jerusalem in AD 70 how did that fulfill this verse? _____
    _____

67. In 1 Thessalonians 4:19, Paul does not want the Thessalonians to "grieve as those who have no hope." What does this mean and how would his teaching spare them from this? _____
    _____

    How does 1 Corinthians 15:17-19 illustrate this? _____
    _____
    _____

68. Explain 1 Thessalonians 4:14. How does Christ's resurrection give reason for faith regarding those who "have fallen asleep in Jesus"?
    _____
    _____

"When Will These Things Be?" : Questions on Eschatology

69. Proponents of the AD 70 Doctrine argue that a spiritual resurrection took place at the destruction of Jerusalem. How does Ephesians 2:4-8 and Colossians 2:11-13 refute this argument? _____
   _____
   _____

70. In a footnote, the author addresses the "gathering" which full preterists argue occurred in AD 70. Summarize how the author refutes this concept. _____
   _____
   _____

71. The author argues that "the reason this language can be used figuratively is that it is grounded in reality." Explain this statement.
   _____
   _____
   _____

   Is this an accurate conclusion? Why or why not? _____
   _____

72. Read 1 Corinthians 15:57-58. How does a belief in a future bodily resurrection allow the believer to accomplish this? _____
   _____
   _____
   _____

Does the Bible Teach the "Rapture," the Coming of an Antichrist, and the Battle of Armageddon?

Mark Mayberry addressed three issues significant to the false doctrine of premillennialism: the so-called "rapture," the coming of an Antichrist figure, and a predicted future battle of Armageddon. After a brief summary of premillennialism, the author addresses these three topics in distinct sections.

1. What does the word "premillennialism" indicate about the beliefs of those who accept it? _____

   _____

   When did this word come into common usage? _____
   How does this contrast to "postmillennialism"? _____

   _____

   How does this contrast to "amillennialism"? _____

2. List some religious groups that teach premillennialism. _____

   _____

   _____

   _____

   List some religious leaders that promote premillennialism. _____

   _____

   _____

   _____

"When Will These Things Be?" : Questions on Eschatology

3. From the author's quote from France, explain the two types of premillennialism and the three types of dispensational premillennialism.
   1. Classical: _____
   _____
   _____
   _____
   _____

   2. Dispensational: _____
   _____
   _____
   _____
   _____

      1. Pretribulational: _____
      _____

      2. Midtribulational: _____
      _____

      3. Posttribulational: _____
      _____

4. Explain the views of dispensational premillennialists regarding the Jews and the church during the millennial. _____
_____
_____
_____

   How do nondispensationalists explain the land promises to Israel?
   _____
   _____
   _____
   _____
   _____

Does the Bible Teach "Rapture," an Antichrist, and Armageddon?

5. What must premillennialists argue are distinct from one another?
   _____

6. List the biblical refutations the author provides to five major tenets of premillennialism.
   1. _____
   2. _____
   3. _____
   4. _____
   5. _____

7. How does Ephesians 3:8-11 demonstrate that the church was not an afterthought? _____

8. Explain the author's argument about the implications of the view that human being could thwart the purposes of God. _____

9. How does Isaiah 53:3-5 demonstrate God's foreknowledge that Jesus would be rejected? _____

10. In Matthew 16:16-19 what two things are equated? _____

11. Explain how the passages offered by the author demonstrate the following assertions he makes.
    The church and the kingdom are composed of the same individuals (Acts 20:28; 1 Pet. 1:18-19; Rev. 5:9-10). _____

"When Will These Things Be?" : Questions on Eschatology

Both realms are accessed through baptism (John 3:1-5; Acts 2:38-40, 46-47; 1 Cor. 12:13; Gal. 3:27-29). _____
_____
_____
_____

The spiritual communion of the Lord's Supper, which believers share each Lord's day, occurs only within a kingdom context (Acts 2:42; 20:7; 1 Cor. 10:16-17; 11:23-26). _____
_____
_____
_____

12. What does Luke 17:20-21 teach about the nature of the kingdom?
_____
_____
_____

13. Read Acts 2, Psalm 2, Isaiah 2, and Daniel 2 and note how these Scriptures connect the church and the kingdom. _____
_____
_____
_____
_____

14. What does Matthew 24:36 teach about knowledge of when Christ will return? _____
_____
_____

15. How does the dictionary define the word "rapture"? _____
_____
_____
_____
_____

Does the Bible Teach "Rapture," an Antichrist, and Armageddon?

16. What is the concept of "the Rapture" in premillennial thought? ___
   _____
   _____
   _____

17. About what do premillennialists disagree when it comes to their teachings on this so-called "Rapture"? _____
   _____
   _____

18. In the author's quote from Pope, explain his argument regarding Matthew 24:30-31. _____
   _____
   _____
   _____

19. Read 1 Thessalonians 4:13-18 from the four translations provided in the book and answer the following questions from the text.
   Who are "those who sleep in Jesus"? _____
   _____

   What appears to be the concern Paul is writing to counter? _____
   _____

   How is the word "prevent" in the King James Version, translated in the other versions? _____
   What three things are said to come "with" the Lord descending from heaven? _____
   _____

   What precedes saints being "caught up"? _____
   _____
   _____

"When Will These Things Be?" : Questions on Eschatology

How is this synonymous with the Christ bringing with Him "those who sleep in Jesus"? _____
_____
_____

Who are those "caught up"? _____
_____
_____

Is this described as a hidden or secret thing? Explain your answer.
_____
_____
_____

How long after this does Paul say they will "be with the Lord"?
_____

What benefit to those in Thessalonica were these words intended to offer? _____

20. In 1 Thessalonians 4:14, to what facts about the gospel does Paul appeal? _____
_____
_____

How do these facts bolster a confidence in what will happen when Christ returns? _____
_____
_____

21. Proponents of the AD 70 Doctrine argue that the events described in 1 Thessalonians 4:13-18 occurred when the Romans destroyed the city of Jerusalem in AD 70. What do you see in the text which refutes that idea?_____
_____
_____

How is that view similar to the premillennial view of "the Rapture"?
_____
_____
_____

Does the Bible Teach "Rapture," an Antichrist, and Armageddon?

22. Make note of what the following Scriptures teach about antichrists.
    1 John 2:18: _____

    1 John 2:22: _____

    1 John 4:3: _____

    2 John 7: _____

23. From the author's quote from *Nelson's New Illustrated Bible Dictionary*, how do men define "the Antichrist"? _____

24. What is the literal meaning of the word "antichrist"? _____

25. Explain the significance of the author's quote from Morris contrasting opposition rather than a claim to be Christ. _____

26. In the period between the Testaments what did Antiochus Epiphanes do? _____

27. What was Paul's warning in Acts 20:29-30? _____

28. Read 2 Thessalonians 2:1-12 and list what is said about this "man of sin." Is he ever called "the Antichrist"? _____

"When Will These Things Be?" : Questions on Eschatology

29. Read Revelation 12-14 and list what is said about the "beast." Is it ever called "the Antichrist"? _____
   _____
   _____
   _____
   _____

30. For what do antichrists "battle"? _____
   _____

31. List some of those whom different teachings have tried to identify as the Antichrist during the following time periods.
   The first century:_____
   _____
   _____

   AD 590-604: _____
   _____

   AD 1143-1241: _____
   _____

   AD 1215-1250: _____
   _____

   The Reformation: _____
   _____
   _____

   Twentieth and twenty-first centuries:_____
   _____
   _____
   _____

   What conclusions should we draw from the fact that there have been so many false identifications? _____
   _____
   _____
   _____

32. In what Scripture does the word "Armageddon" appear? _____
   _____

Does the Bible Teach "Rapture," an Antichrist, and Armageddon?

How is it described in this text? _____
_____
_____

33. From what two Hebrew words is the name "Armageddon" formed and what is the meaning of each? _____
_____
_____

34. What are some possible identifications of "the mountain of Megiddo"? _____
_____
_____

35. Describe the geography of the city of Megiddo. _____
_____
_____
_____

36. Summarize the history of the city of Megiddo. _____
_____
_____
_____

37. What do 1 Kings 9:15-19 and 10:26-29 record about Megiddo? _____
_____
_____

38. Explain the author's point about the symbolism of places such as Waterloo or the Alamo. _____
_____
_____
_____

"When Will These Things Be?" : Questions on Eschatology

39. Describe events associated with Megiddo and the following people or situations.

   Deborah and Barak: _____
   _____

   Gideon: _____
   _____

   King Saul: _____
   _____

   Josiah: _____
   _____

   How might these events have established a particular symbolism in Jewish thought associated with Megiddo? _____
   _____
   _____

40. Under what circumstances was the book of Revelation written?
    _____
    _____
    _____

41. What is the meaning of the Greek word *nikaō* and how often is it used in the New Testament? _____
    _____

    How often is it used in Revelation? _____

42. What is the significance of the phrase used at the beginning and end of the book of Revelation—"shortly come to pass" (Rev. 1:1; 22:6)?
    _____
    _____
    _____

43. What is the significance of identifying Revelation as an apocalyptic book? _____
    _____
    _____
    _____
    _____

Does the Bible Teach "Rapture," an Antichrist, and Armageddon?

44. Summarize the context in which the book of Revelation refers to "Har-Mageddon." _____
_____
_____

45. Explain the author's interpretation of the significance of the reference to Armageddon. _____
_____
_____
_____

   Do you agree with this interpretation? Why or why not? _____
_____
_____
_____

46. Write a brief explanation of the failed predictions made by the following people.
   William Miller: _____
_____
_____

   Charles T. Russell: _____
_____
_____

   Herbert W. Armstrong: _____
_____
_____

   Hal Lindsey: _____
_____
_____

"When Will These Things Be?" : Questions on Eschatology

Willie Day Smith: _____
_____
_____
_____

Ted Kresge: _____
_____
_____
_____

Bill Maupin: _____
_____
_____
_____

Edgar Whisenant: _____
_____
_____
_____

Elizabeth Claire Prophet: _____
_____
_____
_____

Jerry Falwell: _____
_____
_____
_____

Harold Camping: _____
_____
_____
_____

47. What does Deuteronomy 18:15-22 teach about how those should be viewed whose predictions fail?_____
_____
_____
_____

Does the Bible Teach "Rapture," an Antichrist, and Armageddon?

48. How are deceivers described in 2 John 7-11 and how are the faithful to react to them? _____
   _____
   _____

49. Make note of the Lord's warnings about falling prey to deception in the following passages.
   Matthew 24:5: _____
   _____

   Matthew 24:11: _____
   _____

   Matthew 24:24: _____
   _____

   What do these warnings teach about the attitude the faithful should have? _____
   _____

50. What does Isaiah 44:6-8 teach about God's power to know the future? _____
   _____
   _____

   If someone truly spoke from God would their prediction fail? ____

Tough Questions

Does the Bible Teach an End of This Universe?
    Chris Reeves

What Is the Focus of the Mount of Olives Discourse?
    Kyle Pope

When Was Revelation Written and Why Does It Matter?
    Daniel H. King, Sr.

"When Will These Things Be?"
Questions on Eschatology

Does the Bible Teach an End of This Universe?

The first essay examining difficult questions was written by Chris Reeves considering whether biblical teaching indicates an end of the present material universe. The author begins with an overview of three basic truths regarding heaven and the present universe. The essay ends with an examination of erroneous teaching on this subject and two valuable appendices.

1. List the three truths the author asserts in answer to the question posed in the title of this essay.

    1. _____

    2. _____

    3. _____

2. What does Jesus affirm in Matthew 24:35? _____

3. What does Peter teach in 2 Peter 3:10? _____

4. What is the Greek word translated "pass away" in Matthew 24:35 and 2 Peter 3:10 and how is it defined? _____

"When Will These Things Be?" : Questions on Eschatology

5. Read the following passages and note what each says about the universe and its fate.
   Genesis 8:22: _____

   Matthew 5:18: _____

   2 Corinthians 4:18: _____

   Hebrews 1:10-12: _____

6. How do Jehovah's Witnesses and some modern Bible scholars argue that 2 Peter 3:10 should be translated? _____

   List the two Greek words and their meaning upon which this controversy rests and which translations choose which word.
   1. _____

   2. _____

   Explain the author's explanation of the textual issues involved in this question. _____

7. Proponents of the AD 70 Doctrine argue that "heavens and earth" in 2 Peter 3 is an idiomatic way of describing Old Covenant Israel. Read the entire chapter noting how these words are used throughout the chapter. Do you find elements within the text that disprove their theory? _____

Does the Bible Teach an End of This Universe?

8. List things to which the word "heaven" can be applied in the following passages.
   Luke 12:56: _____
   Matthew 6:26: _____
   Matthew 16:2-3: _____
   Luke 17:24: _____
   Matthew 24:30: _____
   Luke 4:25: _____
   Matthew 24:29: _____
   Matthew 5:16: _____
   Matthew 18:10: _____
   1 Peter 3:22: _____

9. Some argue that eternal life will be given on a renovated version of the present earth in a renovated version of the present universe. Explain the significance of the author's list of biblical promises said to be "in heaven" and its ramifications to this argument. What passages in this list do you find the most compelling? _____
   _____
   _____
   _____
   _____
   _____

10. How is the Greek word *ouranios*, translated "heavenly" defined?
    _____
    _____
    _____

    If New Testament writers intended to express that eternal life was "earthly" what word would we expect to find and what does it mean?
    _____
    _____
    _____
    _____

"When Will These Things Be?" : Questions on Eschatology

11. In a footnote in the essay, the author quotes several writers who believe in a future renovated earth but call it "heaven." List some ways they use confused language in making their arguments. _____

12. How do advocates of a restored earth try to explain away the many "in heaven" or "heavenly" passages applied to eternal life? _____

   What do you think about this argument? What weaknesses do you see in it? _____

13. Read John 14:2-3 and make note of what it indicates about the place where the saved with reside. _____

   In a footnote, the author addresses the argument some make that the preparation of Jesus in this verse concerns the establishment of the church. Summarize the author's refutation of this view. _____

   Read John 14:16-18, 23; 15:4-10. Is this addressing the same thing as John 14:2-3? Why or why not? _____

Does the Bible Teach an End of This Universe?

14. How does Matthew 5:34-35 demonstrate that heaven and earth are two separate places? _____
_____

15. How is the authority of Jesus described in Matthew 28:18? _____
_____

    How does this demonstrate that heaven and earth are two separate places? _____
_____

16. Summarize the author's quote from Moore and make note of any biblical problems you see with this view. _____
_____
_____
_____

17. How does Thayer define the word translated "forerunner" in Hebrews 6:20? _____
_____

    What does this indicate about the location of eternal life? _____
_____

18. Summarize the point of the author's quote from Erickson. Have you ever heard people express this mindset? _____
_____
_____

19. In what ways do you see the biblical descriptions of heaven as limited in contrast to the "exaggerated imagination" (as the author puts it) of modern writers? _____
_____
_____
_____

"When Will These Things Be?" : Questions on Eschatology

20. How did Paul describe what he was allowed to see in his vision of the "third heaven" or "Paradise" (2 Cor. 12:2-4)? _____
_____
_____

21. Summarize the caution offered in the author's quote from Summers. Do you agree that this is a danger? _____
_____
_____
_____

22. Read the following Scriptures and make note of the important aspect about salvation emphasized in each.
Philippians 1:23: _____
_____

2 Corinthians 5:8: _____
_____

Revelation 21:3: _____
_____

Revelation 22:4: _____
_____

Revelation 22:23: _____
_____

23. What two biblical facts does the author suggest must be considered in interpreting the meaning of Peter's promise of "new heavens and a new earth" (2 Pet. 3:13)?
   1. _____
   _____
   2. _____
   _____

24. What does Revelation 21:1 and 4 teach about the present heavens and earth following final judgment? _____
_____
_____

Does the Bible Teach an End of This Universe?

25. What do the following lexical sources say about the meaning of the Greek word *aperchomai*, translated "passed away" in Revelation 21:4?
    BAGD: _____
    Zerwick and Grosvenor: _____
    Thayer: _____
    _____
    Liddell and Scott: _____
    _____

26. What words do new creation eschatologists frequently add to their comments on Revelation 21:2, about the new Jerusalem coming down out of heaven? _____
    What problem does Revelation 21:1 pose to this insertion? _____
    _____
    _____

27. Explain the statement that "The Bible begins (Gen. 1:1) and ends (Rev. 21:1) with the creation of a dwelling place (heavens and earth) for His people, first earthly, then heavenly." _____
    _____
    _____
    _____

28. What do Jehovah's Witnesses teach about the "great multitude" and the 144,000? _____
    _____
    _____

29. What do millennialists believe about the earth during their 1,000-year Messianic reign? _____
    _____
    _____

30. List the various views the author explains that are held by different advocates of realized eschatology (or the AD 70 Doctrine). _____
    _____
    _____
    _____
    _____

"When Will These Things Be?" : Questions on Eschatology

31. From the author's citations, what do the following full-preterists say about the afterlife, heaven and hell, and the universe?

    Max King: _____
    _____
    _____

    Samuel Dawson: _____
    _____
    _____

    Don K. Preston: _____
    _____
    _____

32. New creation eschatology is a theory growing in popularity among some scholars that is very similar to the position Jehovah's Witnesses have long taught regarding the universe and eternal life. List the names of some scholars the author cites who accept this view. ____
    _____
    _____
    _____
    _____
    _____

33. Among those associated with churches of Christ who are adopting new creation eschatology, to what two factors does the author attribute their acceptance of this view? How does the author refute this?_____
    _____
    _____

34. In a footnote, from what apocryphal (or pseudepigraphical) book does the author quote as an example of a belief in a restored earth in antiquity? What does it claim? _____
    _____
    _____
    _____

Does the Bible Teach an End of This Universe?

Why shouldn't we accept this in support of this theory? _____
_____
_____

35. Explain the concepts of afterlife in the following religions.
    Baha'i: _____
    _____
    _____

    Hinduism and Buddhism: _____
    _____

    Orthodox Judaism: _____
    _____

    Reformed Judaism: _____
    _____

    Islam: _____
    _____

    How do these differ from biblical teachings? _____
    _____
    _____

36. From the author's quote from Shermer, summarize how many unbelievers, skeptics, and atheists conceive of heaven on earth. What do you see in the teaching of Jesus and the apostles that demonstrates this was not what they were teaching? _____
    _____
    _____
    _____

37. Define "environmentalism." _____
    _____
    _____

"When Will These Things Be?" : Questions on Eschatology

38. Explain how environmentalism could become an important idea for advocates of the following religious views.
    Premillennialism: _____
    _____
    _____

    Jehovah's Witnesses and Seventh Day Adventism: _____
    _____
    _____

    Realized eschatology: _____
    _____
    _____

    New creation eschatology: _____
    _____
    _____

39. Read Romans 8:21. How might advocates of a restored earth interpret this text? _____
    _____
    _____

    In light of the context and our study in this essay how do you think it should be understood? _____
    _____
    _____

40. Summarize the author's argument relating good stewardship of our bodies and in marriages to the attitude Christians should have toward the environment. Can you think of other similar things that require good stewardship that will pass away in the age to come? _____
    _____
    _____

41. How does 2 Peter 3:7 answer the fears of those who imagine that "global warming" or "climate change" could one day destroy life on earth? _____
    _____
    _____

Does the Bible Teach an End of This Universe?

Can one be a good steward of the environment without accepting such fears? Why or why not? _____
_____
_____

42. In 2 Peter 3:11-12, what personal challenge does Peter call the reader recognize in light of the future destruction of this universe? _____
_____
_____

    What similar challenge does Jesus offer after declaring that heaven and earth will "pass away" (Matt. 24:35, 42, 44)? _____
_____

43. Where did Paul declare the hope of a Christian is laid up (Col. 1:5?)
_____

    Upon what does he then challenge the brethren to set their minds (Col. 3:1-2)? _____
_____

44. From the first appendix, summarize the six arguments the author offers that are made by advocates of new creation eschatology.

    1. _____
    _____
    _____

    2. _____
    _____
    _____

    3. _____
    _____
    _____

    4. _____
    _____
    _____

    5. _____
    _____
    _____

"When Will These Things Be?" : Questions on Eschatology

6. _____
_____
_____

45. Does 2 Peter 3 describe the future destruction of the universe with fire as a "type" or "antitype" of the flood? _____
What does Peter identify as an antitype of the flood (1 Pet. 3:21)?
_____

46. List the three periods of time mentioned 2 Peter 3.
2 Peter 3:5: _____
2 Peter 3:7: _____
2 Peter 3:13: _____

47. How does Peter appeal to the power of "the word of God" relative to these time periods in 2 Peter 3:5 and 7? _____
_____
_____

Is Peter comparing the effects of the flood and final judgment by fire or the power and promise of God's word? _____
_____
_____

48. What word is used in 2 Peter 3:10 and 12 of what God will do to the heavens and earth with fire that was not used of its destruction with water? _____

49. In 2 Peter 3:4, to what were mockers appealing to cast doubt on the "promise of His coming"? _____
_____

Does this infer anything about the expectation of what would happening when Christ does return? _____
_____
_____

50. Read the following passages and make note of what each says about fire then determine if all are discussing the same fire.
1 Peter 1:7: _____
_____

Does the Bible Teach an End of This Universe?

1 Peter 4:12: _____
_____

2 Peter 3:7-10: _____
_____
_____

What words are found in 1 Peter 1:7 and 4:12 that are not found in 2 Peter 3:7-10? _____
_____

51. From the context, how can we know that 2 Peter 3 is describing literal fire? _____
_____

52. Some have tried to argue that the "elements" mentioned in 2 Peter 3:10 and 12 are either elementary teachings of false teachers or the elementary principles of the Mosaic Covenant. What do you see in the context that refutes these ideas? _____
_____
_____
_____

53. Even if we set aside the question of whether 2 Peter 3:10 should read "burned up" (KJV, ASV, NASB, NKJV) or "laid bare" (NIV)—"exposed" (ESV), what do we find in 2 Peter 3:7-13 that makes it clear that complete destruction by fire is being described? _____
_____
_____
_____

54. Explain the force of the word "new (*kainos*)" in the passages below and consider how this impacts the argument that the "new (*kainos*)" heavens and earth of 2 Peter 3:13 are just new in quality.
Matthew 9:17: _____
_____

"When Will These Things Be?" : Questions on Eschatology

2 Corinthians 5:17: _____

Hebrews 8:8, 13: _____

Revelation 21:2: _____

55. Read the following passages and make note of what each promises considering whether any of them promised a renewed version of the present heavens and earth.
Isaiah 65:17: _____

Isaiah 66:22: _____

Revelation 21:1: _____

2 Peter 3:13: _____

56. Summarize the eight lessons the author urges us to take away from a study of 2 Peter 3.
   1. _____
   2. _____
   3. _____
   4. _____
   5. _____
   6. _____
   7. _____
   8. _____

What Is the Focus of the Mount of Olives Discourse?

In this essay Kyle Pope takes on the challenging question of whether the discussion Jesus had with His disciples on the Mount of Olives only concerned the destruction of Jerusalem or a future Final Judgment and the destruction of the universe. To explore this question the essay considers differences found in the Gospel accounts and surveys the use and meaning of the word *parousia*, translated "coming" in this text. The reader is encouraged to see the Appendix in this study guide for two additional essays by this author pertinent to this same question.

1. What are three possible answers to the question posed in the title of this essay?
   1. _____
   2. _____
   3. _____

2. Which possibility does author of this essay accept? _____

3. In accepting this view, what two questions does the author explore in this essay?
   1. _____
   2. _____

4. Which view does the author accept? _____

"When Will These Things Be?" : Questions on Eschatology

5. Where is the most extensive account of the Mount of Olives Discourse found? _____
   What passages in Mark and Luke record accounts of the same incident? _____
6. Identify the five elements of this discourse recorded in Matthew that are not included in the shorter accounts in Mark and Luke.
   1. Matthew 24:37-44: _____

   2. Matthew 24:45-51: _____

   3. Matthew 25:1-13: _____

   4. Matthew 25:14-30: _____

   5. Matthew 25:31-46: _____

7. Identify five similar teachings from Luke that Jesus taught on other occasions and make note of the context of each and the text in Matthew to which each is similar.
   1. Luke 17:23-24, 37: _____

      Context: _____
      Similar to: _____
   2. Luke 17:26-36: _____

      Context: _____
      Similar to: _____
   3. Luke 12:41-46: _____

      Context: _____
      Similar to: _____
   4. Luke 12:35-38: _____

What Is the Focus of the Mount of Olives Discourse?

Context: _____
Similar to: _____
5. Luke 19:11-27: _____
_____

Context: _____
Similar to: _____
8. Do differences in biblical accounts of the same incident constitute errors or contradictions in the text? Why or why not? _____
_____

9. Do shorter accounts demand that we interpret longer accounts as synonymous to them in every detail? Why or why not? _____
_____

How do the accounts of Jesus's teaching on marriage, divorce, and remarriage in Matthew 19 and Mark 10 illustrate this? _____
_____
_____

10. How must a belief in the inspiration of Scripture influence conclusions we draw on such issues? _____
_____

11. Look at Matthew 21:23-24:1 and note a few things that happened before Jesus had this discourse with His disciples. _____
_____
_____

12. Identify things that may have motivated the disciples' comments about the temple.
    1. Mark 12:41-44; Luke 21:1-4: _____
    _____
    2. Matt. 23:38-39: _____
    _____

"When Will These Things Be?" : Questions on Eschatology

13. Who are the only disciples specifically identified as involved in this discussion (Mark 13:3)? _____

14. Why is an understanding of the scope of the disciples' question (or questions) at the beginning of this discourse important in understanding its focus? _____
_____

15. What element of the disciples' question is included by Matthew, Mark, and Luke? _____

16. Why does the context of this question (or questions), as seen in Matthew 24:2, Mark 13:2, and Luke 21:6, demand that we understand at least part of the focus of this as addressing the destruction of Jerusalem? _____
_____

17. Although English translations don't make this as apparent, what is the next element of the question (or questions) translated by the author from the Greek in all three account? _____

    What two things does the conjunction of these two elements by the word "and" lead the author to conclude are being asked?
    1. _____
    2. _____

18. How does Luke express the "sign" element of the disciples' question? _____

19. How is Mark's wording slightly different? _____

    List two things Mark records immediately before that the author suggests may be included in this difference.
    Mark 12:40: _____
    Mark: 12:25 _____
    _____

What Is the Focus of the Mount of Olives Discourse?

20. List the two parts of Matthew's wording of the "sign" element of the question.
    1. _____
    2. _____

21. List the four other times that Matthew uses the phrase "end of the age" and note what is said in each example.
    Matthew 13:39 and 40: _____
    _____
    _____

    Matthew 13:49: _____
    _____

    Matthew 28:20: _____
    _____

22. Some have argued that "end of the age" refers to the end of the Jewish age. Do the examples above challenge this conclusion? _____
    _____
    _____
    _____

    Have the just and the unjust already been separated? _____
    _____
    _____

23. In the author's quote from Whiteside, how does Whiteside understand the word translated "coming" in Matthew's wording—of movement and direction or presence and location? _____
    _____
    _____
    _____

24. What is the Greek word translated "coming" in Matthew 24:3?
    _____
    From what two words is it formed and what do they mean?
    1. Word: _____
       Meaning: _____
    2. Word: _____
       Meaning: _____

153

"When Will These Things Be?" : Questions on Eschatology

25. In English, what are some examples of participles? _____
    _____

26. What is the literal meaning of the Greek participle *ousia*? _____
    _____

    What is the literal meaning of the Greek noun *parousia*? _____
    _____

27. Read the following Scriptures in which *parousia* is used and list who or what is described as "being beside" someone or some thing.
    Philippians 2:12: _____
    _____

    2 Corinthians 10:10: _____
    _____

    1 Corinthians 16:17: _____
    _____

    2 Corinthians 7:6-7: _____
    _____

    Philippians 1:26: _____
    _____

    In each of these examples if the person or thing was not actually present would the use of *parousia* even make sense in these passages?
    _____
    _____

28. From the examples the author cited from Greek Literature, list below how each author used the word *parousia*.
    Thucydides:_____
    _____

    Aeschylus: _____
    _____

    Euripides: _____
    _____

    Sophocles:_____
    _____

    In these examples, is it describing a literal or figurative presence?
    _____

What Is the Focus of the Mount of Olives Discourse?

29. In examples the author cited of Greek writers using *parousia* of the presence of good or bad things, and chance or misfortune is *parousia* used of a figurative or actual presence of these things? _____

30. Why is it important to consider the evidence for the use and meaning of the word *parousia*? _____

    How do the conclusions we draw influence our understanding of the focus of the Mount of Olives Discourse? _____

31. What problem does the author illustrate from the titles and approach of two books written by advocates of the AD 70 Doctrine? _____

    How does the author illustrate this problem with the issue of baptism? _____

32. What are the two ways *parousia* was used as a technical term?
    1. _____
    2. _____

33. This first technical use may parallel its use in the Olivet Discourse. Why might that be? _____

34. In a footnote within the essay, the author quotes Dawson's assertion that *parousia* can speak of "visitations of royalty, either personally, or through his chosen representative." Explain why the author disputes this claim? _____

_____

35. Advocates of the AD 70 Doctrine believe that the *parousia* of Jesus was accomplished in the destruction of Jerusalem by the Roman general Titus. The Jewish historian, Josephus records the Roman siege of Jerusalem. Ironically, to whom does he apply the word *parousia*? _____

Did Josephus call this a *parousia* of the Lord? _____

36. The second technical use of the term *parousia* had religious application among both Jews and Greeks. When used of God or pagan gods, was the writer describing what was believed to be an actual or figurative presence of deity? _____

37. The author claims the reference Josephus makes to the incident recorded in 2 Kings 6:17 is the only possible example he has found of *parousia* possibly being applied in a figurative manner of God's presence. What two facts does the author say should be recognized?

1. _____

2. _____

38. What three words from the disciples' question (or questions) are important to note throughout the discourse to interpret its focus?

1. _____
2. _____
3. _____

39. Identify things in the following passages that Jesus says would happen that are not a "sign" and that do not signal "the end."
Matthew 24:5: _____
Matthew 24:6-7a: _____
Matthew 24:7b: _____

What Is the Focus of the Mount of Olives Discourse?

What does He call these things (Matt. 24:8)? _____
_____

40. What is already referenced in Matthew 24:6 that challenges the view that nothing before 24:34 refers to Final Judgment? _____
_____
_____

41. What are some other things Jesus says will happen that are not a "sign" and do not signal "the end" (Matt. 24:9-12)? _____
_____
_____

42. Identify the two times after this that Jesus refers to "the end."
Matthew 24:13: _____
_____

What "end" do you think this describes? _____
Matthew 24:14: _____
_____
_____

What "end" do you think this describes? _____

43. What is the first thing pertinent to their question that Jesus says they would see (Matt. 24:15)? _____
_____

What were they to do when they saw it (Matt. 24:16)? _____
_____

How does Luke describe this (Luke 21:24)? _____
_____
_____
_____

44. With what OT prophet does Jesus specifically connect the phrase "abomination of desolation" (Matt. 24:15)? _____
How does this prophet use this phrase and what is the context?
_____
_____
_____
_____

"When Will These Things Be?" : Questions on Eschatology

45. What does the historical book of 2 Maccabees record about the incident prophesied? _____
_____
_____
_____

46. Is Jesus pointing to the same event prophesied in Daniel or something like it that would happen once again? _____
_____

47. Where does Eusebius say that Christians fled when Jerusalem was destroyed? _____

48. In Matthew's account, where is the first use of *parousia* after the disciples' question? _____
How does this use relate to the verses that immediately precede it?
_____
_____

    If this applied to an unseen figurative coming in the destruction of Jerusalem would that have been unmistakable like lightning? Why or why not? _____
_____

49. What false doctrine, with its attempts to ascertain cosmological events as signs, does the author fear may have led us to conclude that the events described in Matthew 24:29-31 must be taken figuratively? _____

50. What are some biblical examples of cosmological language being used figuratively? _____
_____
_____

51. What three questions does the author urge us to ask about whether this language is figurative in Matthew 24:29-31?
    1. _____
    _____
    2. _____
    _____

What Is the Focus of the Mount of Olives Discourse?

3. _____
   _____

52. Later, in this same discourse, how is some of this same language used (Matt. 25:31)? _____
   _____

   Is this describing AD 70? Why or why not? _____
   _____
   _____

53. How is similar language used in the same book as Jesus stands before the High Priest (Matt. 26:64)? _____
   _____

   Is this describing AD 70? Why or why not? _____
   _____
   _____

54. What preposition do both Matthew and Mark use showing the relationship in time between the "Abomination of Desolation" and the "Son of Man coming on the clouds"(Matt. 24:29; Mark 13:24)?
   _____

   Does this preposition equate the "Abomination of Desolation" and the "Son of Man coming on the clouds" or show these are different events in time? _____
   _____

55. According to Matthew 24:33, would that generation "see" all the things mentioned in verses 33 and 34? _____
   Can unseen things then be included within the things to which 24:34 applies? Why or why not? _____
   _____
   _____
   _____

"When Will These Things Be?" : Questions on Eschatology

56. To what did the phrase "all these things" apply in Matthew 23:36? _____
_____

    Did it include everything He had discussed during the entire day of teaching within the temple? _____

57. Although all of the gospel writers record the "sign" element of the disciples' question (or questions) only Matthew records Jesus answer of a "sign" in connection with Christ's coming. No "sign" will precede it, but what does Matthew 24:30 say the "sign" will be? _____
_____
_____
_____

58. Identify how *parousia* is used in the following passages from Paul's letters to the church in Thessalonica.
    1 Thessalonians 2:19: _____
    _____

    1 Thessalonians 3:13: _____
    _____

    1 Thessalonians 4:15: _____
    _____

    1 Thessalonians 5:23: _____
    _____

    2 Thessalonians 2:1-2: _____
    _____

    2 Thessalonians 2:8: _____
    _____

    2 Thessalonians 2:9: _____
    _____

59. List six things associated with the *parousia* of the Lord described between 1 Thessalonians 4:15 and 5:23.

    1. _____
    _____

    2. _____
    _____

What Is the Focus of the Mount of Olives Discourse?

3. _____

4. _____

5. _____

6. _____

Were all these things accomplished in AD 70? Why or why not?
_____
_____
_____

60. In 2 Thessalonians 2:8 and 9 *parousia* is used of Christ's coming then the coming of the "man of lawlessness." While there are many questions about who the "man of lawlessness" is, most see him as a literal being, literally present upon earth. Is it consistent to apply *parousia* literally in one verse but figuratively of Christ in the verse that precedes it? Why or why not? _____
_____

61. To what does Peter's first use of *parousia* refer (2 Pet. 1:16)? _____
_____

   In the same epistle, he then speaks of Christ's promised *parousia* (2 Pet. 3:4). Is it reasonable to imagine that Peter uses this term literally in the first chapter but figuratively in the third chapter? Why or why not? _____
_____

62. Both Peter and Paul speak of Jesus's Second Coming "as a thief in the night" (2 Pet. 3:10; 1 Thess. 5:2). The first time this figure is used is in the Mount of Olives discourse (Matt. 24:43-44). Do you think this could be the basis for Peter and Paul's teaching? Why or why not?
_____

"When Will These Things Be?": Questions on Eschatology

Is it reasonable to apply the first use of this language to AD 70 but the later uses to Jesus's Second Coming? Why or why not? _____
_____
_____

63. List some things that the author's quotes from early Christian writers such as Ignatius and Justin indicate about what these Christians immediately after the New Testament was written understood about the Second Coming of Jesus and the meaning of *parousia*. _____
_____
_____

Did they believe it had already happened? _____
Did they apply *parousia* to AD 70? _____

64. What does the author's final quote from Justin illustrate about what Christians immediately after the New Testament understood about the meaning of *parousia* when applied to Christ's Second Coming?
_____
_____

65. How do the words of Matthew 25:13 summarize well the overall theme of the Olivet Discourse? _____
_____

When Was Revelation Written and Why Does It Matter?

The book of Revelation is God's final inspired text on issues pertaining to eschatology. In this essay, Daniel H. King, Sr. explores the question of its dating and why the timing of its composition matters in questions about end times events. He considers evidence from early church writers and ancient history, then examines problems with some theories regarding its date.

1. What are some things mentioned in the book of Revelation that could be taken literally or figuratively depending on whether it was written before or after AD 70? _____
   _____
   _____

2. Depending upon its date, what two political leaders may be described in chapter 13 of the book? _____
   _____

3. List how the city, called "Babylon the Great" in chapters 17-18, is generally identified by each view.
   Early date:_____
   Late date:_____

4. What practice was not allowed in Jerusalem at the time of its destruction? _____
   _____

   What is a chief accusation against the evil city of the book of Revelation (17:1, 2, 4; 18:3, 9; 19:2)? _____
   _____

"When Will These Things Be?" : Questions on Eschatology

Does this have bearing on how we identify the city? _____
_____
_____

5. Explain the author's statement, "if the dating is wrong, the symbols are wrong?" _____
_____
_____

6. How can the dating of the book of Revelation provide an open door to the concepts of radical preterism? _____
_____
_____

7. Does everyone who believes in an early date accept full-preterism? _____

   What is the author's caution regarding this? _____
_____
_____

8. How do advocates of full-preterism view texts recording the Olivet Discourse? _____
_____

   What events do advocates of this view believe happened in AD 70?
_____
_____

9. According to the author, what is absent from writings in the early church? _____
_____

   How can this be explained if the New Testament taught full-preterism? _____
_____
_____

When Was Revelation Written and Why Does It Matter?

10. What does Revelation 22:20 declare? _____
_____
_____

   How must this verse be interpreted in light of respective views of dating the book?
   Early date: _____
   _____

   Late date: _____
   _____

11. When did Irenaeus live? _____
   Where was he born? _____
   Who did he hear and see as a child? _____
   _____

   What is significant about him? _____
   _____
   _____

12. Why is this information about Irenaesus significant to any comments he might make about the book of Revelation? _____
   _____
   _____

13. When does Irenaeus date the writing of the book of Revelation?
   _____

   What church historian affirmed the same claim? _____
14. When did Tertullian of Carthage live? _____
   How did he describe Domitian? _____
   _____

   How did he describe John's time on Patmos? _____

15. When did Clement of Alexandria live? _____
   What did he write about when John left Patmos? _____
   _____

   How did Eusebius identify the "tyrant" to which Cement refers?
   _____

"When Will These Things Be?" : Questions on Eschatology

How did Clement describe John after his time on Patmos? _____

Would this description be as accurate if Revelation was written before AD 70? _____

16. What did Eusebius write about how long John lived? _____

    What did He write about why John left Patmos? _____

    What does he call the source of his claims about John? _____

17. Around what time did Victorinus of Pettau live? _____

    What did he write? _____

    Summarize what he claimed about John's time on Patmos and his writing of the Apocalypse (i.e. the book of Revelation)? _____

18. When did Jerome live? _____

    What did he write about the writing of Revelation? _____

19. What does the author assert about those who claimed it was written during the time of Claudius or Nero? _____

When Was Revelation Written and Why Does It Matter?

20. When did Domitian reign? _____
    How was his early reign characterized? What are some highlights?
    _____
    _____

21. What were some early efforts he made to raise public morality?
    _____
    _____
    _____

22. How does the Roman historian Suetonius describe Domitian's upbringing? _____
    How must this be understood? _____
    _____

23. Who was Domitian's father? _____

24. What did Tacitus and Suetonius believe about Domitian's interest in literature? _____
    _____

25. How did Cassius Dio describe Domitian's personality? _____
    _____

26. Describe Domitian's relationship with his wife, Domitia Logina.
    _____
    _____
    _____

27. How was Domitian's paranoia demonstrated? _____
    _____
    _____
    _____

28. Describe the events leading to Domitian's death. _____
    _____
    _____

"When Will These Things Be?" : Questions on Eschatology

29. According to Suetonius, how did Domitian insist on being addressed? _____

30. On what charge did Domitian have Flavius Clemens executed? _____

    Who do some think Flavius Clemens may have been? _____

31. Pandateria was the name of an island off the coast of Italy. Who did Domitian banish there? _____

32. In what year did Domitian's persecution of Christians begin? _____

33. Read Revelation 1:9 and list how John describes the reason he was on Patmos. _____

34. Describe how the letters between Pliny the Younger and Trajan describe trials of Christians around AD 111-113. _____

35. What does the author suggest about similarities between this process and what likely happened to John? _____

36. What does Eusebius claim about the island of Patmos? _____

When Was Revelation Written and Why Does It Matter?

37. Describe what is known about the martyrdom of the early Christian named Ignatius. _____
   _____
   _____
   _____

38. What is measured in Revelation 11:1-2? _____
   Do you see indicators within the text as to whether this should be taken literally or symbolically of some spiritual reality? If so, what do you see? _____
   _____

39. According to the author, rather than the Herodian temple, what does he argue bears more similarity to what is described in Revelation 11? _____

   What do you think leads him to this conclusion? _____
   _____

40. List everything that is said about the city mentioned in Revelation 11:8. _____
   _____
   _____
   _____

41. Explain the author's interpretation of this description. _____
   _____
   _____
   _____
   _____
   _____

"When Will These Things Be?" : Questions on Eschatology

42. In the essay, the author argues that Revelation 17:18 is describing the same city. How is the city described in this passage? _____
_____
_____

Would this description be applicable to Jerusalem in the time of either Nero or Domitian? Why or why not? _____
_____
_____

43. What was the estimate of Tacitus about the size of Jerusalem in the 60s? _____

44. How does the author define the Latin phrase *princeps urbium*? ____
_____

How did Aristides describe Rome? _____

45. The author cites numerous ancient writers and their descriptions of Rome. What does this demonstrate? _____
_____
_____

46. What does Revelation 1:7 foretell? _____
_____

Rather than Final Judgment, what do some argue that this is describing? _____
_____

47. How to some try to connect Revelation 1:7 and Zechariah 12:12?
_____
_____

Read Zechariah 12:9-14. How does the mourning in this text differ from the mourning in Revelation 1:7? _____
_____
_____
_____

170

When Was Revelation Written and Why Does It Matter?

Notice how the Gospel of John uses Zechariah 12:10 in John 19:37. Based on this, who is the "Him" in Zechariah 12:10 for whom they are said to mourn? _____
Is this the same occasion for and cause of mourning foretold in Revelation 1:7? Why or why not? _____
_____
_____
_____

48. Read the passages below and identify whether Jewish or Gentile "tribes" are being described.
    Genesis 12:3: _____
    Genesis 28:14: _____
    Psalm 71:17: _____
    Zechariah 14:17: _____
    Revelation 5:9: _____
    Revelation 7:9: _____

49. List the seven hills upon which the ancient city of Rome sat:
    1. _____ 2. _____
    3. _____ 4. _____
    5. _____ 6. _____
    7. _____

50. What was the *Septimontium* festival and what does its name mean?
    _____
    _____

51. What do the ancient nicknames for Rome, *heptalophos* (Greek) and *septicollis* (Latin) mean? _____

52. What is pictured on the back of the Roman coin known as a *sestertius* minted in AD 71? _____
    _____
    _____

"When Will These Things Be?" : Questions on Eschatology

What similarities does this bear to what John describes in Revelation 17:1-9? _____
_____
_____

53. List the seven hills which advocates of an early date associate with ancient Jerusalem:

    1. _____ 2. _____
    3. _____ 4. _____
    5. _____ 6. _____
    7. _____

    Using a Bible atlas or Bible dictionary find a map of ancient Jerusalem. Are any of these hills outside of the city walls? If so, which ones (cf. Acts 1:12)? _____
    _____
    _____

54. What is the earliest preserved reference we have in ancient literature to Jerusalem sitting on "seven hills"? _____
    _____
    _____

55. With what hill is Jerusalem usually identified? _____

56. How many hills did Josephus associate with Jerusalem? _____
    _____
    _____

57. Is there evidence from ancient history that the actual city of Babylon sat on seven hills? _____

58. Explain the challenges faced by both early and late dating when it comes to identifying the seven kings. _____
    _____
    _____
    _____
    _____
    _____
    _____

When Was Revelation Written and Why Does It Matter?

59. Why does the author lean towards identifying Nero as the first of the seven? _____
_____

60. In both Hebrew and Greek, letters and numbers have a numerical correspondence. How do many commentators interpret the meaning of the number 666 in Revelation 13:18? _____
_____

61. What are some difficulties with interpreting this as referring to Nero?
_____
_____
_____
_____

62. What was Domitian's full name? _____
_____

63. Explain the author's argument if 666 is a reference to Nero, but as a type of the kind of persecutor whom Domitian would imitate (cf. Rev. 13:3, 12). _____
_____
_____
_____

64. To the church in what city is Revelation 2:8-11 addressed? _____
_____

In a letter written in the second century by Polycarp to the church in Philippi, he discusses Paul's inspired letter to the Philippians. What does he say about the church in Smyrna (his hometown) when Paul wrote Philippians? _____
_____

65. When Philippians was written Paul was imprisoned (Phil. 1:13). If we argued that this was his Caesarean imprisonment, what is the earliest date the author suggests we could assign to the establishment of a church in Smyrna? _____
What is the latest possible date? _____

"When Will These Things Be?": Questions on Eschatology

Read Revelation 2:8-11 and consider what impact Polycarp's claim has on the date of Revelation. _____

66. How is the church in Laodicea described in Revelation 3:17? _____

   What happened to the city of Laodicea in AD 60/61? _____

67. Read Revelation 3:14-23. If Revelation was written under Nero's persecution of Christians (AD 64 and following) does the wording of Revelation 3:14-23 sound like it describes a city possibly only four years after being devastated by an earthquake? Explain your answer.
   _____

68. How is this evidence less problematic for a late date view of Revelation? _____

69. How widespread was the persecution of Christians under Nero in AD 64? _____

   Is there any evidence it affected Asia Minor? _____
70. How widespread was the persecution of Christians under Domitian some thirty years after Nero? _____

71. What evidence of persecution do you see in the book of Revelation? How widespread does it appear to have been? _____

When Was Revelation Written and Why Does It Matter?

Does this evidence lend support to an early or late date for the book of Revelation? Explain your answer. _____
_____
_____

72. Read the following passages the author cites as examples of references to worship of the emperor in the book of Revelation. Note what each says about such worship.
    13:4, 8, 12, 15: _____
    14:9, 11: _____
    16:2: _____
    19:20: _____
    20:4: _____
    21:8: _____
    22:15: _____

73. What did the Roman emperor Caligula build for himself in Rome and compel Romans to do? _____
_____

    What did he try to set up in the temple in Jerusalem? _____
_____

74. When was the first temple of worship of the Roman emperor built in Pergamum? _____
    What statement in Revelation 2:13 might refer to emperor worship in this city? _____
_____

75. From the author's quote from Friesen, when was the temple in Ephesus for worship of the Flavian family (i.e. Vespasian, Titus, and Domitian) dedicated? _____

76. When did emperor worship start to be bound upon those living in Roman provinces? _____
_____

"When Will These Things Be?": Questions on Eschatology

If Revelation is describing widespread compulsion toward emperor worship, how does the answer to the previous question impact the dating of the book? _____

77. Was Nero's persecution of Christians because of their failure to participate in emperor worship? _____

78. Explain the author's argument that the "holy city" of Revelation 11:1-2 must refer to the church rather than the physical city of Jerusalem. _____

79. Read Revelation 11:19. What does John see within the temple? _____

    What challenge does this pose to interpreting this as the physical temple in Jerusalem? _____

    What does this passage say about where the temple shown to John was? _____

80. Write out the full quote penned by Irenaeus around AD 180, about when Revelation was written. _____

    Why does the author argue we can confidently accept this claim? _____

Personal Eschatology: Men's Track

Where Are the Dead?
　Jesse Flowers

Does the Bible Teach Purgatory?
　Daniel Dow

Does the Bible Teach Reincarnation?
　Steve Wallace

"When Will These Things Be?"
Questions on Eschatology

Where Are the Dead?

Jesse Flowers wrote the first essay of men's studies on the question of the state of the dead following life upon earth. He begins with a survey of the nature and reality of death then explores Jesus's teaching in Luke 16 on the Rich Man and Lazarus. From this and co-related texts, he concludes by refuting various erroneous doctrines taught about death.

1. Why does Ecclesiastes 7:2 say that the "house of mourning" is a better place to go than the "house of feasting"? _____
   _____

2. What are the Hebrew and Greek names for the place of the dead?
   Hebrew: _____
   Greek: _____
   What does the Greek word mean? _____

3. Explain the phrase "gates of sheol" from Isaiah 38:10. _____
   _____
   _____

4. In Psalm 16:10, what part of human beings does David say goes to this place? _____
   How does Peter interpret this passage in Acts 2:27-31? _____
   _____
   _____

5. In this text, what words does Peter show describe the same place?
   _____
   _____

6. In 1 Corinthians 15:55, Paul paraphrases Hosea 13:14. Explain Paul's wording in relation to the text of Hosea. _____
   _____
   _____

"When Will These Things Be?" : Questions on Eschatology

7. In the context of 1 Corinthians 15:54-55, what does Paul teach robs hades of its victory? _____
   _____

8. According to Hebrews 9:27, what two appointments must all people keep? _____
   _____

9. What power does the Preacher, in Ecclesiastes 8:8, indicate is lacking to all men? _____
   _____

10. Some argue that Ecclesiastes 9:5 teaches that the soul passes out of existence upon death. How would you answer this assertion? _____
    _____
    _____
    _____

11. In Genesis 2:16-17, what did God warn would be the consequence of sin? _____
    How was this warning realized? _____
    _____

12. Both Romans 5:12 and 1 Corinthians 15:21-22 discuss the effect of Adam's sin on mankind. Look at the context of each and answer the following questions:
    1. Are both passages talking abut the same type of death? If so, how would you prove this? If not, what demonstrates this? _____
       _____
       _____
       _____
       _____

    2. How did Adam pass either type of death on to his descendents?
       _____
       _____
       _____
       _____

Where Are the Dead?

13. Based on James 2:26 and Ecclesiastes 12:7, what things are separated upon physical death? _____

    How does Ecclesiastes 3:19-21 describe this separation? _____
    _____
    _____

14. In Ecclesiastes 9:11-12, in discussing death, what does the Holy Spirit lead the Preacher to say happens to all? _____
    _____

    Explain what that means. _____
    _____

15. What does James say our attitude should be toward each day of life and future plans we make (Jas. 4:13-15)? _____
    _____

16. The Hebrew writer describes humans as being held in bondage through the fear of death (Heb. 2:14-15). What does that mean?
    _____
    _____

    What does the Hebrew writer also say about the effect of Jesus coming to earth? _____
    _____
    _____

17. In Luke 23:43, where did Jesus tell the thief they both would be after they died? _____
    Based on Peter's words in Acts 2::27-31, what does that tell us about this place? _____
    _____
    _____

"When Will These Things Be?" : Questions on Eschatology

18. In Matthew 22:31-32, Jesus quotes Exodus 3:6. What point does He make from this? _____
   _____

   How does this concern the resurrection? _____
   _____

19. List some differences Paul describes in 2 Corinthians 5:1 between the Christian's life now and what awaits us. _____
   _____
   _____

20. According to Revelation 14:13, what may now be said of those who "die in the Lord"? _____
    How does this verse end that may explain why this is true?_____
    _____

21. Some have dismissed Luke 16:19-31 by saying it is a parable. Does the passage identify this account as a parable? _____
    If it is a parable, does that mean that what it says about hades is fictional? Why or why not?_____
    _____
    _____

    What would it indicate about the honesty of Jesus if He led people to believe in conditions after death that are only imaginary and not real?_____
    _____
    _____

22. Summarize Luke 16:19-31 in your own words. _____
    _____
    _____
    _____
    _____
    _____

Where Are the Dead?

23. In Luke 16:22, what phrase is used to describe the portion of hades where Lazarus was taken? _____

    How does this compare to what we have already seen in Luke 23:43 and Acts 2:27-31? _____
    _____

24. What is the definition given in *Strong's Greek Dictionary* for "paradise"? _____
    _____

25. In his essay, how does the author use the following texts to show that paradise is not always equivalent to heaven?
    John 20:17: _____
    _____

    Psalm 16:8-11: _____
    _____

    Acts 2:31: _____
    _____

26. Some advocates of the AD 70 Doctrine argue that sheol and hades always describe a state that is gloomy and undesirable. What challenges does Luke 16:19-31 pose to this view? _____
    _____
    _____

27. In Luke 16:23-24, how is the location of the rich man described? _____

    What does he experience there? _____
    _____

28. What did he request from Abraham? _____
    _____
    _____

"When Will These Things Be?" : Questions on Eschatology

29. List two reasons his requests are denied.
    1. _____
       _____
    2. _____
       _____

30. In the quote from Colly Caldwell in the essay, how does Caldwell explain the rich man's "reward"? _____
    _____

31. What is said to separate the two regions within hades (Luke 16:26)? What function does it appear to serve? _____
    _____

    How does Caldwell explain its significance? _____
    _____

32. The Roman Catholic Church teaches that souls guilty of unforgiven *venial* (i.e. "forgivable") sins may go to purgatory upon death to be purged of sin and ultimately obtain eternal life with God. Answer these question from your study of Luke 16:19-31.
    1. Is hades "purgatory"? Why or why not? _____
       _____
       _____
       _____

    2. Can one in hades change his or her condition? How does the answer to this question influence the previous question? _____
       _____
       _____
       _____

33. List five things the author cites in his essay as proof that the dead are conscious after death.
    1. _____
       _____
    2. _____
       _____

Where Are the Dead?

3. _____

4. _____

5. _____

34. How does 2 Corinthians 5:10 reinforce that it matters how we live our lives before God? _____

35. According to Psalm 116:15, what is "precious" in the sight of God? _____

    Explain what this means. _____

36. What is the difference between hades and hell? _____

    What about Matthew 10:28 demonstrates a difference? _____

37. Some struggle to understand how the dead are separated in hades but Final Judgment has not yet occurred. How do the following passages address this?
    John 5:28-29: _____

    Matthew 25:31-46: _____

    Romans 2:1-11: _____

    Romans 14:10-12: _____

    2 Corinthians 5:10: _____

"When Will These Things Be?" : Questions on Eschatology

39. How is the term "eschatology" defined? _____

    What is the doctrine of "realized eschatology"? _____

40. List the six things this doctrine argues happened in AD 70.
    1. _____
    2. _____
    3. _____
    4. _____
    5. _____
    6. _____

41. What does Revelation 20:13-14 teach about hades and when does it indicate that this will happen? _____

    What does this text also say about death? _____

    If death continues, can we argue that this has already happened? _____

42. In the author's quote from Willis, how does he argue that this has not yet occurred? _____

43. How does Jesus's teaching about the rich man and Lazarus refute the error of materialism (i.e. the doctrine that man is only flesh and blood)? _____

44. How does John 5:29 demonstrate that the dead are presently in hades? _____

45. According to Revelation 20:12-15, when will hades be cast into the "lake of fire"? _____

Does the Bible Teach Purgatory?

The second essay on personal eschatology was jointly written by a husband and wife—Daniel and Diana Dow. Their essay and the following study questions are featured in both the men's and women's tracks of this series. Their essay defines the terms used by advocates of this doctrine. Then examines its history and biblical passages used to argue for its presence in biblical teaching.

1. Define so-called "mortal sins." _____
   _____
   _____

   What three things must be involved in "mortal sins"?
   1. _____
   _____
   2. _____
   _____
   3. _____
   _____

2. Define so-called "venial sins." _____
   _____

3. What is "purgatory"? _____
   _____

   How do the definitions of sins defined above play a role in the concept of purgatory? _____
   _____
   _____
   _____

"When Will These Things Be?" : Questions on Eschatology

4. List the three religions that believe in purgatory.
   1. _____
   2. _____
   3. _____
5. Is the word "purgatory" found in the Bible? _____
6. In the authors' quote from Striving, from what ancient religion was the concept of purgatory borrowed? _____

7. What two Greek philosophers held to concepts like purgatory?
   1. _____
   2. _____
8. How might pagan concepts have perverted biblical concepts about sheol or hades resulting in a belief in purgatory? _____
_____
_____

9. Name the first Roman Catholic leader who shows signs of teaching a concept of purgatory and when he lived. _____

10. What was the purpose of the letter written by Innocent IV to those in Greece? _____
_____

11. What did the Second Council of Lyon do in 1274? _____
_____

To what did the Eastern Orthodox churches object? _____

List two points this council argued.
1. _____
2. _____

Does the Bible Teach Purgatory?

12. What did the Council of Trent order? _____
_____
_____

13. In the quote the authors' offer from the book, *Beginning Apologetics: How to Explain and Defend Catholic Faith,* is there any advice offered that would be good for all Bible students to practice? _____
_____

    Where would you disagree with advice from the book? _____
_____

14. Summarize Matthew 5:25-26: _____
_____

    How do those who believe in purgatory try to use this passage in support of their belief? _____
_____

    Do you see problems with their argument? _____
_____

15. How do the authors' refute this use of the passage? _____
_____

    What is not mentioned in this passage? _____
_____

16. Summarize Matthew 12:32: _____
_____

17. How did pope Gregory the Great argue that this passages supports a belief in purgatory? _____
_____

"When Will These Things Be?" : Questions on Eschatology

In the quote from Gibbons, how does he argue from this same passage? _____
_____

Do you see any problems with these arguments? _____
_____
_____

18. How do the authors' refute these ideas? _____
_____
_____

Does the fact that there is no sin in heaven and the declaration that a sin from earth cannot be forgiven in the age "which is to come" necessarily infer a place after life where sin can be forgiven short of heaven? Why or why not?_____
_____
_____

What is not mentioned in this passage? _____
_____

19. Summarize 1 Corinthians 3:15: _____
_____
_____

How did pope Gregory use this passage? _____
_____
_____

Do you see any problems with this argument? _____
_____
_____

20. What is the context of 1 Corinthians 3:15? _____
_____
_____

How does this relate to its interpretation? _____
_____

Does the Bible Teach Purgatory?

21. In the context what "work" is being considered? _____

    How then may this "work" endure or be burned up? _____

22. In the authors' quote from Willis, how does he explain this? _____

23. How do the authors' relate this to Ezekiel 3:19? _____

    What is not mentioned in 1 Corinthians 3:15? _____

24. Summarize 1 Peter 3:18-20: _____

    How do advocates of purgatory use this passage? _____

    Do you see any problems with their use of this? _____

25. What two places are described in the hadean realm?
    1. Name: _____
       How is this described? _____

    2. Name: _____
       How is this described? _____

    How does this differ from what its proponents teach about purgatory?

"When Will These Things Be?" : Questions on Eschatology

26. How does Hebrews 9:27 describe man's appointments? _____
_____

27. In the historical book of 2 Maccabees 12:44-45, what does it record Jews doing in the period between the Old and the New Testaments?
_____
_____
_____

    What does the book, *Beginning Apologetics,* argue about this passage from 2 Maccabees? _____
    _____
    _____

28. List some religions that pray for the dead. _____
_____
_____

29. 2 Maccabees is part of the Apocrypha. What is the Apocrypha?
_____
_____

    How has it been viewed throughout history? _____
    _____
    _____

30. Does evidence that something was practiced in history necessarily mean it was approved by God? Explain your answer. _____
_____
_____

31. What did the Council of Florence declare about prayers for the dead?
_____
_____

32. How is 2 Timothy 1:16-18 used by proponents of a belief in purgatory? _____
_____
_____

Does the Bible Teach Purgatory?

Upon what assumption does this argument rely? _____

What is not mentioned in this text? _____

33. What is the context of 1 Corinthians 15:29? _____

    In this context, explain its meaning. _____

    What do advocates of purgatory argue about this text? _____

    Do you see problems with this argument? _____

34. Read Ecclesiastes 12:13-14 and 2 Corinthians 5:10. According to these passages, for what will we be judged and called to account on the Day of Judgment? _____

    Do these passages pose any challenges to the belief in purgatory? _____

35. What do Romans 5:9 and Ephesians 1:7 teach about how sin is purged from a person's life? _____

    According to the doctrine of purgatory, how is one purged of sins after death? _____

Does the Bible Teach Reincarnation?

The final essay in the men's studies examining personal eschatology was written by Steve Wallace. Through exploring twelve truths about reincarnation, Wallace demonstrates that the concept of souls being reborn into different bodies, is not compatible with biblical teaching.

1. In the beginning of his essay, the author asserts that "reincarnation is not in the Bible." Some have argued that the Bible supports the concept of reincarnation. Can you think of things in the Bible that could be construed to support this concept? _____
   _____
   _____

   How would you show that these things do not support that reincarnation is a reality? _____
   _____
   _____

2. Define "reincarnation" (or "transmigration"). _____
   _____
   _____

3. Define "metempsychosis." _____
   _____

4. According to McClintock and Strong, what is believed to be the only thing that stops the cycle of rebirth? _____
   _____
   _____

   In this teaching, what determine the nature of one's existence in each subsequent life? _____
   _____
   _____

Does the Bible Teach Reincarnation?

5. Reincarnation was born out of Hinduism. The goal of the cycle of rebirth is to ultimately become one with Brahman. From the definition offered in the essay, demonstrate some differences between Brahman and the God of the Bible. _____
   _____
   _____

   Is the New Testament concept of eternal life becoming one with God? Why or why not? _____
   _____
   _____

6. From Young's *Encyclopedia of Hinduism*, define "karma." _____
   _____
   _____

7. How is the so-called "law of karma" believed to affect the cycle of rebirths? _____
   _____

   In science, Newton's Third Law of Motion states, "For every action, there is an equal and opposite reaction." The apostle Paul taught, "Do not be deceived, God is not mocked; for whatever a man sows, that he will also reap" (Gal. 6:7). Are these teaching the "law of karma"? If not, how are they different? _____
   _____
   _____

8. In Genesis 3:4-5, what false promise allured Adam and Eve to sin?
   _____

9. According to 2 Timothy 1:10, what did Jesus accomplish? _____
   _____
   _____

   How does this passage say salvation comes? _____

"When Will These Things Be?" : Questions on Eschatology

10. In John 14:6, how does Jesus teach that one may come to the Father? _____
_____

11. Explain the author's use of Ephesians 4:4-6 to demonstrate that a belief in reincarnation is built on a different belief system than faith in Christ. _____
_____
_____

12. How do the following Scriptures warn against things like reincarnation? Acts 20:28-30: _____
_____

    1 Timothy 4:1-5: _____
    _____

    2 Peter 2:1: _____
    _____

13. List the names of the five ranks in the Indian caste system.
    1. _____
    2. _____
    3. _____
    4. _____
    5. _____

14. In Christ, we are instructed to "remember the poor" (Gal. 2:10) and warned that wealth can hinder a person from going to heaven (Matt. 19:23-24). Under the caste system, one is wealthy because of karma and poor because of karma. That establishes a religious justification for rigid class separation. What are some problems this creates?
_____
_____
_____

    Doesn't that show that this is a man made concept used to keep the poor in their place and elevate the wealthy? _____

Does the Bible Teach Reincarnation?

15. List the three consequences of the law of karma quoted in the essay from Mike Willis and explain each point.

    1. _____
       Explanation: _____
       _____

    2. _____
       Explanation: _____
       _____

    3. _____
       Explanation: _____
       _____

16. How is the teaching of Ecclesiastes 9:10 contrary to the fatalism of reincarnation? _____
    _____

17. Ezekiel 18:20 teaches that one person is not held accountable for the sins of another. How does this conflict with the law of karma? ____
    _____
    _____

18. How is reincarnation a form of salvation through works? _____
    _____
    _____

    Does this conflict with Ephesians 2:8-9? Why or why not? _____
    _____
    _____

19. The Bible teaches about God's justice but also about His grace (see Eph. 2:8-10; Titus 2:11-12). Explain why the author suggests that the law of karma knows nothings about grace, "only the gloom of strict retribution." _____
    _____
    _____
    _____

"When Will These Things Be?" : Questions on Eschatology

20. How do the author's examples of multiple people claiming to be Marie Antoinette or Cleopatra illustrate his claim that someone is "misled, deceived, or lying"? _____
_____
_____

21. What steps have courts in India taken that demonstrates the unreliability of claims of reincarnation? _____
_____

22. What claim did the actress Shirley MacLaine make about her own supposed reincarnation? _____
_____

    Is this claim supported by the historical record? _____

23. List some contradictory and conflicting views that exist among those who believe in reincarnation. _____
_____
_____
_____
_____

24. What does Hebrews 9:27 teach that contradicts reincarnation? _____
_____
_____

25. Does the teaching of Jesus in Luke 16:19-31 show support for the law of karma? Why or why not? _____
_____
_____
_____

26. According to John 9:3 is a person's condition in life the result of actions in a former life? _____

27. When does 2 Corinthians 5:10 teach that a reckoning for deeds committed in the flesh takes place? _____
_____
_____

Does the Bible Teach Reincarnation?

28. In biblical examples of the dead miraculously being brought back to life what is not recorded that is a characteristic of Near Death Experiences (NDE)? (See 1 Kings 17:17-24; 2 Kings 4:18-37; 13:20-21; Mark 5:35-43; Luke 7:11-16; John 11:1-54). _____
   _____
   _____

29. What are some inconsistencies about NDEs that bring their value as evidence into question? _____
   _____

30. In Luke 16:19-31, what facts about the "life time" (v. 25) of Lazarus and the rich man show that reincarnation is not a biblical teaching?
   _____
   _____
   _____

31. Explain the author's point about the singular nature of the "abode of the soul" as demonstrated in the following texts:
   2 Corinthians 5:1, 4: _____
   _____
   2 Corinthians 12:2-3: _____
   _____
   1 Peter 1:13-14: _____

32. How do the following texts about final judgment conflict with the concept of reincarnation?
   2 Corinthians 5:10: _____
   _____
   Matthew 25:14-30: _____
   _____
   Hebrews 9:27: _____
   _____

"When Will These Things Be?" : Questions on Eschatology

33. In the cases of the widow's son (1 Kings 17:22) and Lazarus (John 11) had their souls gone into different bodies? _____
   If so, what would happen to that other body when they were brought back to life? _____
   _____
   _____

34. How does the biblical doctrine of a resurrection of the dead on the Day of Judgment conflict with reincarnation (give Scriptures with your answer)? _____
   _____
   _____
   _____

Personal Eschatology: Women's Track

Where Are the Dead?
  Aleta Samford

Does the Bible Teach Purgatory?
  Diana Dow

Does the Bible Teach Reincarnation?
  Jennifer Maxey

"When Will These Things Be?"
Questions on Eschatology

Where Are the Dead?

Aleta Samford begins the women's track on issues addressing personal eschatology. The author relates her personal experience in facing the death of her husband and how that forced her to confront what the Bible teaches about the state of the dead prior to Final Judgment. Her essay surveys biblical teaching on the issue, offering three arguments demonstrating that the dead do not go to heaven or hell prior to Final Judgment.

1. Have you ever lost loved ones in your life whose passing caused you to wonder where they are? What were your thoughts at that time?
   _____
   _____

2. It is common to hear people describe loved ones who have died in faithfulness to the Lord as "in heaven." Do you think they always mean their loved one is already in heaven or are they describing where they believe they will ultimately go?_____
   _____
   _____

3. List some answers you have heard to the question posed in the title of this article? _____
   _____

   Do you think this is an important question to consider? Why or why not?_____
   _____
   _____

"When Will These Things Be?" : Questions on Eschatology

4. What are some dangers that could result from confusion over this question? _____
_____
_____

5. How is God described in Hebrews 12:9? _____
_____

6. To what part of us does our creation in God's "image" refer (Gen. 1:26)? _____

7. In Zechariah 12:1, what is God said to form within man? _____
_____

8. According to Ecclesiastes 12:7, upon death what happens to our spirit and body respectively? _____
_____
_____

9. What does Paul tell Christians "we know" about what happens when our bodies, "our earthly house" is destroyed (2 Cor. 5:1)? _____
_____

10. What did David say about his child who died and his own future (2 Sam. 12:23)? _____
_____

    What are some things this tells us about the state of the dead? ____
_____
_____

11. Some fear cemeteries imagining that the souls of the dead stay with their bodies. What do the following Scriptures teach us about this?
    Genesis 35:18: _____
_____

    James 2:26: _____
_____

12. What problem plagues all accountable souls (Rom. 3:23)? _____
_____
_____

Where Are the Dead?

13. How may one receive remission of this problem (Mark 16:16; Acts 2:38)? _____

14. What leads to righteousness and salvation (Rom. 10:9-10)? _____

15. Under what condition may one be said to have "both the Father and the Son" (2John 9b)? _____

16. Some teach that once a person is in Christ it is impossible to sin in such a way as to lose salvation. What does 2 Peter 2:20-22 teach about this? _____

17. What does John say results if one departs from the "doctrine of Christ" (2 John 9a)? _____

18. What two appointments await all souls (Heb. 9:27)?
    1. _____
    2. _____

19. According to Luke 23:43, where did Jesus go when He died? _____

20. How do we know that the criminals crucified with Jesus actually died (John 19:31-33)? _____

21. How can we know from John 20:17 that Jesus did not go to heaven when He died? _____

"When Will These Things Be?" : Questions on Eschatology

22. When did He ascend into heaven (Acts 1:9-11)? _____
    _____

23. Read Luke 16:19-31 and answer the following questions about conditions of the dead:
    What is the name of the place where all are said to go? _____
    How is the place where the rich man went described? _____
    _____

    What is the place where Lazarus went called? _____
    _____

    How are these places separated? _____
    _____

    Is travel permitted between these places? _____
    Is a change in one's condition possible? _____
    _____

    Is contact with the living (generally) permitted? _____

24. Using Revelation 21:8, how does the author argue that the rich man is not in hell?_____
    _____
    _____
    _____

25. According to Revelation 20:11-12, who stands before God's throne at the Judgment?_____
    _____

    Had this taken place yet in the account of the rich man and Lazarus? _____

26. What three words are translated "hell" in the King James Version?
    1. _____
    2. _____
    3. _____

26. What word is used in Revelation 20:12-15? _____
    _____
    _____

Where Are the Dead?

From this passage, how can we know that the word the KJV translates "hell" is not referring to the place of eternal punishment? ____

27. According to Revelation 20:13-15, from where had the dead who stand before the throne come? ____

What happens to this place after the dead are judged? ____

If the rich man and Lazarus went to this place, had their judgment occurred yet? ____

27. Summarize what the following Scriptures teach about the place called *gehenna*.
Matthew 5:32: ____

Mark 9:43: ____

Luke 12:5: ____

28. What is the only verse where the word *tartarus* is used? ____

Who is said to be there? ____

According to this passage, had these already faced judgment? ____

29. What is the Hebrew word that corresponds to the Greek word *hades*? ____

30. According to Acts 2:27 and 31, where did Jesus go when He died? ____

Comparing this with Luke 16 and the words of Jesus on the cross, what can we conclude about the place Jesus calls "paradise"? ____

"When Will These Things Be?" : Questions on Eschatology

31. What Old Testament text is quoted in Acts 2:27? _____
    _____

32. In Luke 16:27-31, what did the rich man ask for his brothers? _____
    _____
    _____
    _____

    Was it allowed? _____

33. Some have argued that in the account Jesus offers in Luke 16 He was making a moral point by utilizing mythological concepts commonly accepted by Jews and Greeks, but was not describing a real place. From our study, what problems do you see with that argument?
    _____
    _____
    _____
    _____

34. Read 1 Thessalonians 4:13-18 and make note of what it says about the dead at Christ's Second Coming. _____
    _____
    _____
    _____
    _____

35. According to 2 Peter 3:10, what will happen on the "day of the Lord"? _____
    _____
    _____

36. What does Paul say will happen to those who have died before Judgment Day when Christ returns (1 Thess. 4:16)? _____
    _____
    _____

37. What does Paul say will happen to those who are still alive when Christ returns (1 Thess. 4:16)? _____
    _____
    _____

Where Are the Dead?

38. What transformation does Paul describe in 1 Corinthians 15:50-53? _____

39. Some have struggled to understand how, if souls are already separated in hades, the judgment has not already occurred. How might the author's description of Final Judgment as "the passing of eternal sentence on the resurrected dead" help overcome this struggle? _____

    In this life, what happens to violent criminals before their trial? _____

40. What did Jesus say would happen at the resurrection (John 5:28-29)? _____

    If the dead went directly to heaven or hell upon death would this have happened yet? _____

41. What is the "last enemy" that will be destroyed (1 Cor. 15:26)? _____

    According to 1 Corinthians 15:54-55, when this happens, what else will occur? _____

    Have these things happened yet? _____

42. What may now be said of those who "die in the Lord" (Rev. 14:13)? _____

43. What does Peter teach the Lord's delay in returning for judgment demonstrates (2 Pet. 3:9-12)? _____

Does the Bible Teach Purgatory?

The second essay on personal eschatology was jointly written by a husband and wife—Daniel and Diana Dow. Their essay and the following study questions are featured in both the men's and women's tracks of this series. Their essay defines the terms used by advocates of this doctrine. Then examines its history and biblical passages used to argue for its presence in biblical teaching.

1. Define so-called "mortal sins." _____
   _____

   What three things must be involved in "mortal sins"?
   1. _____
   2. _____
   3. _____

2. Define so-called "venial sins." _____
   _____

3. What is "purgatory"? _____
   _____

   How do the definitions of sins defined above play a role in the concept of purgatory? _____
   _____

Does the Bible Teach Purgatory?

4. List the three religions that believe in purgatory.
   1. _____
   2. _____
   3. _____
5. Is the word "purgatory" found in the Bible? _____
6. In the authors' quote from Striving, from what ancient religion was the concept of purgatory borrowed? _____
7. What two Greek philosophers held to concepts like purgatory?
   1. _____
   2. _____
8. How might pagan concepts have perverted biblical concepts about sheol or hades resulting in a belief in purgatory? _____
_____
_____

9. Name the first Roman Catholic leader who shows signs of teaching a concept of purgatory and when he lived. _____

10. What was the purpose of the letter written by Innocent IV to those in Greece? _____
_____

11. What did the Second Council of Lyon do in 1274? _____
_____

    To what did the Eastern Orthodox churches object? _____
_____

    List two points this council argued.
    1. _____
    2. _____

"When Will These Things Be?" : Questions on Eschatology

12. What did the Council of Trent order? _____
_____
_____

13. In the quote the authors' offer from the book, *Beginning Apologetics: How to Explain and Defend Catholic Faith*, is there any advice offered that would be good for all Bible students to practice? _____
_____

    Where would you disagree with advice from the book? _____
_____
_____

14. Summarize Matthew 5:25-26: _____
_____
_____

    How do those who believe in purgatory try to use this passage in support of their belief? _____
_____
_____

    Do you see problems with their argument? _____
_____
_____

15. How do the authors' refute this use of the passage? _____
_____
_____

    What is not mentioned in this passage? _____
_____

16. Summarize Matthew 12:32: _____
_____
_____

17. How did pope Gregory the Great argue that this passages supports a belief in purgatory? _____
_____
_____

Does the Bible Teach Purgatory?

In the quote from Gibbons, how does he argue from this same passage? _____

Do you see any problems with these arguments? _____

18. How do the authors' refute these ideas? _____

Does the fact that there is no sin in heaven and the declaration that a sin from earth cannot be forgiven in the age "which is to come" necessarily infer a place after life where sin can be forgiven short of heaven? Why or why not? _____

What is not mentioned in this passage? _____

19. Summarize 1 Corinthians 3:15: _____

How did pope Gregory use this passage? _____

Do you see any problems with this argument? _____

20. What is the context of 1 Corinthians 3:15? _____

How does this relate to its interpretation? _____

"When Will These Things Be?" : Questions on Eschatology

21. In the context what "work" is being considered? _____

    How then may this "work" endure or be burned up? _____
    _____

22. In the authors' quote from Willis, how does he explain this? _____
    _____
    _____

23. How do the authors' relate this to Ezekiel 3:19? _____
    _____

    What is not mentioned in 1 Corinthians 3:15? _____
    _____

24. Summarize 1 Peter 3:18-20: _____
    _____
    _____

    How do advocates of purgatory use this passage? _____
    _____

    Do you see any problems with their use of this? _____
    _____

25. What two places are described in the hadean realm?
    1. Name: _____
       How is this described? _____

    2. Name: _____
       How is this described? _____

    How does this differ from what its proponents teach about purgatory?
    _____
    _____

Does the Bible Teach Purgatory?

26. How does Hebrews 9:27 describe man's appointments? _____
_____

27. In the historical book of 2 Maccabees 12:44-45, what does it record Jews doing in the period between the Old and the New Testaments?
_____
_____

What does the book, *Beginning Apologetics,* argue about this passage from 2 Maccabees? _____
_____

28. List some religions that pray for the dead. _____
_____

29. 2 Maccabees is part of the Apocrypha. What is the Apocrypha?
_____
_____

How has it been viewed throughout history? _____
_____

30. Does evidence that something was practiced in history necessarily mean it was approved by God? Explain your answer. _____
_____

31. What did the Council of Florence declare about prayers for the dead?
_____
_____

32. How is 2 Timothy 1:16-18 used by proponents of a belief in purgatory? _____
_____
_____

"When Will These Things Be?" : Questions on Eschatology

Upon what assumption does this argument rely? _____

_____

What is not mentioned in this text? _____

_____

33. What is the context of 1 Corinthians 15:29? _____

_____

In this context, explain its meaning. _____

_____

_____

What do advocates of purgatory argue about this text? _____

_____

_____

Do you see problems with this argument? _____

_____

_____

34. Read Ecclesiastes 12:13-14 and 2 Corinthians 5:10. According to these passages, for what will we be judged and called to account on the Day of Judgment? _____

_____

_____

Do these passages pose any challenges to the belief in purgatory?

_____

_____

35. What do Romans 5:9 and Ephesians 1:7 teach about how sin is purged from a person's life? _____

_____

According to the doctrine of purgatory, how is one purged of sins after death? _____

_____

_____

Does the Bible Teach Reincarnation?

The final essay in the women's track examining personal eschatology was written by Jennifer Maxey and examines whether the Bible teaches reincarnation. Challenging the reader to recognize the pervasive influence of a belief in reincarnation in modern culture, the author challenges women of faith to stand boldly against this false religious belief.

1. What does the Holy Spirit command, through the apostle John in 1 John 4:1? _____

   List four points the author highlights in the verse that follow this that show how to do this.

   1. _____
   2. _____
   3. _____
   4. _____

2. Using the criteria above, how do most religions that believe in reincarnation fare when tested? Explain your answer. _____

"When Will These Things Be?" : Questions on Eschatology

3. Explain the author's summary of what reincarnation is and why she asserts that it is not biblical. _____
_____
_____
_____

4. What was the criticism of the Jews in Romans 10:3? _____
_____

5. In John 5:39-42, was it enough for those whom Jesus was teaching to simply know what was right? _____
   What did they fail to demonstrate? _____
_____
_____

6. What does the author suggest true love demands? _____
_____
_____

7. According to statistics the author cites, what percentage of adults in the U.S. accept reincarnation as a valid belief? _____
   How many of those consider themselves Christians? _____

8. Summarize the results of the author's Facebook survey on reincarnation. _____
_____
_____
_____
_____

   Do you find these results startling? Explain your answer. _____
_____
_____
_____
_____

Does the Bible Teach Reincarnation?

9. What does the author suggest are some aspects of the emotional appeal that a belief in reincarnation has for women? _____

   _____
   _____
   _____

   Have you ever encountered such inquiries into the "soul's journey" in which no one condemns, no one corrects, and no one judges? Explain your experience. _____

   _____
   _____

10. Explain how the passages offered by the author counter the common sayings we might hear or use.
    "Hey Mom, next time I'm born, I hope I'm a butterfly!" (1 John 3:2): _____

    "You must be channeling Grandma today" (Isa. 8:19): _____

    "Oh, wow. Deja Vu! We must have known each other in a past life" (Heb. 9:27): _____

    "Looks like that guy has some bad karma!" (Gal. 6:7): _____

11. List the concepts promoted in the following popular books.
    Conversations with God by Neale Donald Walsch: _____

    _____

    Many Lives, Many Masters by Brian L. Weiss, M.D.: _____

    _____
    _____

"When Will These Things Be?" : Questions on Eschatology

12. In the following children's movies, list the elements relevant to beliefs in reincarnation promoted.
    Moanna: _____
    _____

    Pocahontas: _____
    _____
    _____
    _____

    Brother Bear: _____
    _____

    The Princess and the Frog: _____
    _____

    A Dog's Purpose: _____
    _____

    The Lion King: _____
    _____
    _____

13. What does 2 Timothy 4:5 command? _____
    _____

14. List the twenty-two proponents on reincarnation cited by the author:
    _____   _____   _____
    _____   _____   _____
    _____   _____   _____
    _____   _____   _____
    _____   _____   _____
    _____   _____   _____
    _____   _____

Does the Bible Teach Reincarnation?

15. What hope do various versions of reincarnation offer? _____
    _____
    _____

    How does this differ from the hope in Christ? _____
    _____

16. How does Ephesians 2:19-22 describe the relationship between God, His people, and Christians towards one another? _____
    _____
    _____

17. What are some advantages about a belief in reincarnation that may seem appealing to people? _____
    _____
    _____

    Why do you think faith in Christ is more advantageous? _____
    _____

18. List the four resolutions issued at the conference of American Spiritualists in Providence, Rhode Island in 1866.
    1. _____
    2. _____
    3. _____
    4. _____

    How does 1 Timothy 4:1-3 characterize these types of views? _____
    _____

19. How do modern spiritualists define themselves? _____
    _____
    _____
    _____
    _____

"When Will These Things Be?" : Questions on Eschatology

20. List eight things spiritualists deny.
    1. _____ 2. _____
    3. _____ 4. _____
    5. _____ 6. _____
    7. _____ 8. _____

21. Explain the possible connection the author makes between transgenderism and a belief in reincarnation. _____
_____

22. Following the author's suggestion, consider the perspective you might have on life from the following perspectives. Especially take into consideration challenges you would face in considering faith in Christ.

    Low-born Indian wife and mother, raised in the tradition and values of Hinduism: _____
    _____
    _____

    High-born Thai woman, raised in the tradition and values of Buddhism: _____
    _____
    _____

    Alaskan native of Inuit descent, daughter of the tribal chief, raised in tradition of animism: _____
    _____
    _____

    Middle-class American woman raised in Norway in the tradition of New Age spiritualism: _____
    _____

23. What does Paul affirm about the gospel in Romans 1:16? _____
    _____

24. List some things from which those who converted to Christ in the first century had to turn. _____
    _____
    _____
    _____

Does the Bible Teach Reincarnation?

25. List some things Romans 1:21-32 says that the unbelieving world could know about God. _____
_____
_____

26. Explain how appealing to the following points can help establish "common ground" when trying to teach believers in reincarnation. There is more than meets the eye. _____
_____

    There is a God (or god, or gods). _____
    _____

    There are powers. _____
    _____

    Demons are real and pervasive. _____
    _____

    Angels are real, and sometimes visit. _____
    _____

    The Devil (Satan) is real, active, and aware. _____
    _____

27. What is the warning of 2 Corinthians 6:14-17? _____
    _____

    How does this apply to our efforts to teach others? _____
    _____
    _____
    _____

"When Will These Things Be?" : Questions on Eschatology

28. What is the difference between doctrines of "transmigration" and resurrection? _____

29. What do the following passages teach about the transformation that will take place at the resurrection?
    1 Corinthians 15:44: _____

    2 Corinthians 5:4: _____

    1 Thessalonians 5:23: _____

    Philippians 3:21: _____

30. How does Romans 6:1-4 describe the role baptism plays in being born again into Christ? _____

31. Using the chart from the book, fill-in the blanks.

Superiority of Born Again to Re-Born .... *again*

Born again	vs.	Re-born ... again
Into the heaven-bound body of Christ	**Destination**	Into another earth-bound body
Of water Of spirit	**Nature**	
	Identity "... In Christ, he is a new creature; old this are passed away; behold, all things have become new" (2 Cor. 5:17)	Same essential self
Intentional gift of grace now, answered by intentional good words and deed	**Source**	
Reconciled to God	**State**	Alienated from "god"

Does the Bible Teach Reincarnation?

	Decision "The Lord...is longsuffering toward us, not willing that any should perish, but that all should come to repentance" (2 Pet. 3:9)	
	Judgement	Condemned : repeat cycle
New birth is salvation	**Result**	Re-birth is defeat
	Hope	
	Future "Well done...I will put you over many things; enter into the joy of your Master...but throw out the worthless servant into outer darkness...weeping and gnashing of teeth" (Matt. 25:23,30)	
Look forward and upward for understanding	**Focus**	
	Foundation "Anyone who hears these sayings of mine and does them, I will liken him to a wise man who built his house on the rock" (Matt. 7:24)	Foundation of self
Clear, revealed, answered by God	**Knowledge**	

30. Read 1 Corinthians 15:20-23. What does this text us Christ's resurrection indicates about the future resurrection of the saved?

   _____

   _____

   How does this refute reincarnation? _____

   _____

"When Will These Things Be?" : Questions on Eschatology

31. How do the following passages show that Jesus is the answer to what people are seeking?

    John 14:6: _____

    _____

    John 11:25: _____

    _____

32. List the four final cautions the author offers about the dark side of reincarnation.

    1. _____
       _____

    2. _____
       _____

    3. _____
       _____

    4. _____
       _____

Appendix: General Studies

Does Apocalyptic Language Foreshadow or Exaggerate?
Kyle Pope

Did 2020 Signal the End?
Andrew Dow

Teaching a Future Judgment to the "Nones", David Deason

Is God Cruel to Send Souls to Hell?
David A. Cox

Creation and the End of the World, Jim Deason

"No One Knows" and the Deity of Christ, Mike Willis

Is Matthew 24:34 a Transition Verse?, Kyle Pope

"When Will These Things Be?" Questions on Eschatology

Does Apocalyptic Language Foreshadow or Exaggerate?
By Kyle Pope

Introduction
Apocalyptic language is defined as language "describing or prophesying the complete destruction of the world; resembling the end of the world; momentous or catastrophic; of or resembling the Biblical Apocalypse [i.e., the Book of Revelation]" (*New Oxford American Dictionary*). While such language may draw its name from *apokalupsis,* the Greek name of the Book of Revelation, apocalyptic language is used throughout the Bible. For example, the Holy Spirit led Joel to write, "I will show wonders in the heavens and in the earth: blood and fire and pillars of smoke. The sun shall be turned into darkness, and the moon into blood, before the coming of the great and awesome day of the LORD" (Joel 2:30-31, NKJV). After Christ's ascension, when the Holy Spirit came upon the apostles on the day of Pentecost, Peter declared that these events fulfilled Joel's prophecy. He told the people, "this is what was spoken by the prophet Joel" (Acts 2:16), going on to quote the text from Joel (Acts 2:17-21). While there is no indication that these things literally occurred on that day, Peter's application of Joel's words shows they carried a figurative and spiritual sense as they related to the significance of what happened on that day—the church began, the New Covenant was initiated, and the promised kingdom of the Messiah was established.

"The Voices of the Prophets"
While all would agree that apocalyptic language can have a figurative and spiritual application, the question is if that means we should see all examples of this type of language as figurative and spiritual, but never literal? For advocates of the AD 70 Doctrine (Realized Eschatology or Full-Preterism) the answer is, "Yes!" Don K. Preston, a prolific spokesman for this movement, writes:

"When Will These Things Be?": Questions on Eschatology

> The language of the prophets by its very definition is veiled and obscure; it is marked by poetic imagery, license, and exaggeration, and is impressed with hyperbole, metaphors, and symbols. . . . The manner of fulfillment was essentially spiritual, not physical, and that language which on its face appears to describe the dissolution of the chemical elements in a cataclysmic end of time and space must be given a figurative construction and interpretation. This is required, not only because of the confines for fulfillment imposed by statements of time, but by the *usus loquendi* [manner of speech] of the prophets" ("What Is Preterism").

A favorite appeal of the proponents of this doctrine is Acts 13:27, where Paul rebukes the Jewish leaders in their rejection of Jesus because, "they did not know Him, nor even the voices of the Prophets which are read every Sabbath." To AD 70 proponents, understanding "the voices of the Prophets" doesn't just mean making sound interpretation of the teachings of the Prophets. To them, "the voices of the Prophets" is almost a type of hidden code that allows those who have truly discerned it to realize that Jesus won't really come again, the dead won't literally be raised, the heavens and earth won't really "pass away," and all end-times apocalyptic language will never literally happen.

Does God Exaggerate?

As any who have ever encountered this doctrine know, addressing the claims of this complicated and confusing teaching is a momentous endeavor, well beyond the scope of this short study. For a more thorough treatment of the overall topic, I refer the reader to my study, *Thinking about AD 70: Challenging Realized Eschatology* (Athens, AL: Truth Publications, Inc., 2019). For our purposes, let us explore one simple issue: if all apocalyptic language is "exaggeration" and "hyperbole" wouldn't that compromise the truthfulness of God?

Full-preterists place great emphasis on the truthfulness of God when it comes to time statements. Samuel G. Dawson, for example, writes, "Our God doesn't make time prophecies and then fail to fulfill them. His faithfulness is greater than that" (*Essays on Eschatology*, 28). William Bell echoes this, writing, "To maintain the integrity of the text and the inspiration and truthfulness of Christ, the event has either occurred, or Christ was untruthful. That's the bottom line and simplicity of it all" ("What Is Realized Eschatology?"). Preston further writes, "Time elements cannot

Does Apocalyptic Language Foreshadow or Exaggerate?

be disregarded or explained away consistent with the doctrine of verbal inspiration. The very authority of the Scriptures is at stake" ("What Is Preterism?"). Certainly, God means what He says, but these teachers apply rigid, subjective definitions to terms such as "near" and "at hand," but then gloss over the actual words the Holy Spirit reveals in apocalyptic language. That treats time statements as literal and absolute, but apocalyptic language as "exaggeration."

The Truthfulness of God

In speaking of God, Paul told Titus that He "cannot lie" (Titus 1:2). This principle of God's nature is a theme that runs throughout all of Scripture. In 1 Samuel, we read: "The Strength of Israel will not lie nor relent. For He is not a man, that He should relent" (15:29). The Law of Moses declares, "God is not a man, that He should lie, nor a son of man, that He should repent. Has He said, and will He not do? Or has He spoken, and will He not make it good?" (Num. 23:19).

What bearing should this have on our understanding of apocalyptic language? No, on the day of Pentecost God did not actually cause "wonders in the heavens" or "blood and fire and pillars of smoke." The sun was not actually "turned into darkness" and the "moon into blood," so did God simply exaggerate? If so, how can we know that any of His promises are not simply exaggeration? If so, did God lie? Absolutely not! On the other hand, what if apocalyptic language has an immediate and a future application? In other words, while the apocalyptic cosmological events did not actually happen on Pentecost, did the significance of that event foreshadow an ultimate future reality? If so, God said it, and He will ultimately do it.

If we interpret all apocalyptic language as simply an *usus loquendi* (or manner of speech) of the prophets, consider where that must lead us. Did God mean what He said in affirming that the dead will come forth from graves (John 5:28-29)? Did God mean what He said when He stated "heaven and earth will pass away" (Matt. 24:35)? Did God mean what He said when He promised that Jesus will come on the clouds (1 Thess. 4:17)? Did God mean what He said when He promised that all nations shall be gathered together for judgment (Matt. 25:32)? Did God mean what He said when He promised a time when there will be no death, tears, or pain (Rev. 21:4)?

Advocates of the AD 70 Doctrine treat time statements literally, but all other end-times promises as figurative. That is presumptuous! How does that not impugn the honesty of God? The Holy Spirit asks, "Has He said, and will He not do? Or has He spoken, and will He not make it good?" (Num. 23:19). Yes, God always does what He says. Apocalyptic language is not a divine lie, or an "exaggeration." Even when applied to temporal acts of judgment and significant events, it foreshadows an ultimate reality. God said it; one day He will do it! God has spoken it and He will make it good in the end!

Bibliography

Bell, William. "What Is Realized Eschatology?" *AllThingsFulfilled.com*. October 26, 2008. https://www.allthingsfulfilled.com/what-is-realized-eschatology/.

Dawson, Samuel G. *Essays on Eschatology*, Amarillo, TX: SGD Press, 2009.

Preston, Don K. "What Is Preterism?" *BibleProphecy.com*. Preterist Research Institute. September 18, 2008. https://bibleprophecy.com/articles/2006/09/18/what-is-preterism/.

Did 2020 Signal the End?
By Andrew Dow

Introduction

2020 has come and gone, but the endless barrage of bad news has been seared into our memories. Political and cultural divisions were heightened by a controversial President and heated election cycle. Protests and riots broke out across the nation which resulted in city blocks being burned, police headquarters being attacked, and the US Capitol being invaded. Wild fires ravaged the west coast. "Murder hornets" became commonplace terminology. All the while, Covid-19 spread around the globe claiming lives and livelihoods.

All of this is enough to remind anyone of the divine judgments found in the Bible. Prognosticators seized the opportunity to use these events as signs of Christ's coming and the end of the world.[1] After a year like 2020, we may feel like the world is falling apart. Is it, though? Do the events of 2020 indicate that the end of the world is imminent?

These Events Are Not All That Unique

Discussions concerning 2020's relationship to the last day should be tempered with an appropriate perspective. The events we collectively endured in 2020 were not unique. The world has seen pandemics.[2] Mass death, starvation, and wars have come and gone. Raging forest fires and bug infestations have decimated property and crops. Political unrest and cultural divisions are nothing new. Last year was uncomfortable, but it was not anything that humanity has not already seen.

---

[1] Hagee, John. "Pastor John Hagee: Coronavirus: Dress Rehearsal for the New World Order." *YouTube. Hagee Ministries.* June 28, 2020. https://www.youtube.com/watch?v=H_vNWmqWmZc&ab_channel=HageeMinistries.

[2] Pope, Kyle. "How Christians Responded to Spanish Influenza in 1918." *Focus Online.* April 18, 2020. https://focusmagazine.org/how-christians-responded-to-spanish-influenza-in-1918.php.

"When Will These Things Be?" : Questions on Eschatology

Solomon's reminder is helpful here: "That which has been is that which will be, and that which has been done is that which will be done. So there is nothing new under the sun. Is there anything of which one might say, 'See this, it is new'? Already it has existed for ages which were before us" (Eccl. 1:9-10, NASB95; cf. 3:15; 6:10). What we lived through is not unlike what our ancestors endured. Therefore, the disasters of 2020 are no more an omen of the end of the world than the disasters of previous generations.

Why, then, did 2020 seem so earth-shattering? First, the events of last year seemed egregious because—to be frank—they were! People suffered and died. Livelihoods were lost. While such events are not unique, they were devastating. Second, the events of 2020 seem overwhelming because we were directly affected. They happened to us! It is one thing to read about pandemics, fires, and financial crises in a history book, it is quite another thing to live through them yourself. Third, the events of 2020 seemed like the end because 24/7 news coverage and the near constant connection to social media hype amplified every painful event.

Last year was bad, but the notion that we can only explain it as the inauguration of the end-times is simply not true. Similar tragic events plagued humanity long before 2020. If God allows the world to continue, they will undoubtedly plague mankind again.

Can the End Be Predicted?

This is hardly the first time that current events have been used to predict Christ's return.[3] In recent memory, the blood moon eclipses of 2014 and 2015 were thought to signal the end. Harold Camping predicted the world's end would be in May (and then October) 2011. How many end-time predictions surrounded the turn of the millennium at 1999-2000? The one common theme is that each of these "prophecies" failed. In each of these cases, as Moses reminds us, "the prophet has spoken it presumptuously; you shall not be afraid of him" (Deut. 18:15-22).

The Bible teaches that the timing of the Last Day is unknown. Paul wrote, "You yourselves know full well that the day of the Lord will come just like a thief in the night. While they are saying, 'Peace and safety!'

---

[3] "List of Dates Predicted for Apocalyptic Events." *Wikipedia*. Wikimedia Foundation. February 28, 2021. https://en.wikipedia.org/wiki/List_of_dates_predicted_for_apocalyptic_events.

then destruction will come upon them suddenly" (1 Thess. 5:2-3; cf. 1 Pet. 3:10). The thief analogy highlights the uncertain timing of this event. Thieves do not announce their arrivals in advance, and neither has God.

This uncertainty is intensified by the tension between descriptions of the end being both *imminent* and *distant*. On the one hand, Jesus's return is described as if it is coming shortly. Paul and James both encourage righteous living on the basis that "the Lord is near" (Jas. 5:8; Phil. 4:5; cf. Rev. 22:20). Meanwhile, other texts describe the end as remaining in the distant future. In Matthew 24-25 Jesus tells three parables in which a master "is not coming for a long time" (24:48), a "bridegroom was delaying" (25:4), and a master returned "after a long time" (25:19). Which is it? Both! These are two ways of describing the same event. The end is imminent: it is the next event in God's redemptive plan. The end is also distant: it is yet future, and there are preparations to be made as we wait.

Uncovering the timing of the end is simply not the Bible's concern. God is far more interested in us living in anticipation of that day. This is why every attempt to discern the "signs of the times" in order to predict Christ's return is ultimately futile. These attempts try to discern more than what is revealed in the Bible.

A Reminder That There Will Be an End

Although 2020 will not help us predict the end, it is still useful to remind us that the end is coming. When life becomes "business as usual," we risk neglecting the Bible's eschatological outlook. The suffering of 2020 was not "good," but "good" *can* still come out of it.

The tragedies of 2020 should remind us we live in a world affected by sin. The world as God designed it was "very good" (Gen. 1:31). Adam and Eve lived in a God-made home, ate God-provided food, and lived in unity with God and each other. After they sinned, however, Adam and Eve were evicted, compelled to labor, accused each other, and were separated from God (Gen. 2-3). Because of man's sin, the earth is "cursed" (Gen. 3:17). "The whole creation groans and suffers," Paul says, as it anxiously waits to be "set free from its slavery to corruption" (Rom. 8:19-22). The devastation we witnessed is a vivid reminder of sin's curse.

The tragedies of 2020 should also remind us that God has promised to undo the curse of sin (Gen. 3:15). As we see sin and death run its course, we can take comfort in God's promise to eradicate both. John points to a day when "there will no longer be any curse" (Rev. 22:3). This will be on that last day: "Then comes the end... The last enemy that will be abolished is death" (1 Cor. 15:24-26). We may watch in terror as the world seems to fall apart around us, but we can look on in hope knowing that our God has guaranteed us victory (1 Cor. 15:57).

The events of 2020 will not bring us closer to predicting the day and hour of Jesus's return. However, these events remind us that the end is a reality. Friends, that is good news!

Teaching a Future Judgment to the "Nones"

By David Deason

Introduction

Over the last few decades, the religious world has seen a general decline among its members. For a variety of reasons, people are leaving churches, embracing secularism, and even abandoning their faith in God. This growing number of people have been described by the Pew Research Center, among others, as the "Nones." Those among the "Nones" are generally divided into one of three subgroups: Atheists, Agnostics, and Nothing in Particular. In December 2017, Pew Research conducted a survey to learn more about this growing category of people. The majority of the group cites "I question a lot of religious teachings" as their primary reason for being unaffiliated, followed by "I don't like the positions churches take on social/political issues." When separating the three subgroups, only 8% of the "Nothing in Particular" subgroup claimed "a lack of belief in God" as the most important reason for not having a religious affiliation. This is intriguing! The majority of this subgroup believes in God, but struggles with things that are taught in churches. So how can Christians reach this group of people? How can we help them "connect the dots" concerning the certainty of a future judgment before God, and the necessity of seeking salvation through Jesus Christ?

God Is

Although the majority may believe in an idea of God, it is vital that we begin by proving and reinforcing the fact that God is real. Addressing the brethren in Rome, Paul said, "For since the creation of the world His invisible attributes, His eternal power and divine nature, have been clearly seen, being understood through what has been made, so that they are without excuse" (Rom. 1:20, NASB). When one observes the intricate design of the universe, only foolishness would suggest that its existence is nothing more than an accident. Even with the vast technology available today, no one has designed anything as sophisticated, complicated, and special as this earth and the universe in which it is contained. No one would deny the fact that an exceptional design team accomplished an incredible feat of engineering in their work on a modern computer, smart device, or vehicle. The idea that the latest and greatest smart phone was simply an accident where all the parts fell together in just the right place is ridiculous and laughable. So why would anyone make that argument for this world? The only logical conclusion one can reach is that the Hebrew author was correct when he said, "For every house is built by someone, but the builder of all things is God" (Heb. 3:4).

God Has Spoken

Solidifying the reality of God then leads to teaching that He has not been silent. The Lord revealed Himself to Adam in the garden. Enoch walked with Him. He spoke with Noah. He delivered His law to Moses and the people of Israel. He appointed judges, kings, and prophets. The Lord revealed His will through all of these avenues. God has always wanted mankind to communicate with Him, to know His will and to choose to follow Him. Ultimately, this is the reason Jesus came to the earth—to be the perfect manifestation of God's desire to commune with humanity. The Hebrew letter opens, "God, after He spoke long ago to the fathers in the prophets in many portions and in many ways, in these last days has spoken to us in His Son, whom He appointed heir of all things, through whom also He made the world" (Heb. 1:1-2).

Modern skeptics seek to minimize and devalue the Bible. However, is it logical to believe in a God who is powerful enough to design and create the entire universe and all it contains, but lacks the power to preserve His words through the years? No! Still, skeptics argue that God did not know what conditions would evolve in the future, and if He were to rewrite the Bible today, He would say things differently and not be as harsh concerning certain topics. Yet, the Lord tells us that "I am God, and there is no other; I am God, and there is no one like Me, declaring the end from the beginning, and from ancient times things which have not been done, saying, 'My purpose will be established, and I will accomplish all My good pleasure'" (Isa. 46:9-10). When God said, "Let there be light" (Gen. 1:3), He knew everything that would take place from that moment all the way to the end of time, even things yet to happen. Nothing has

Teaching a Future Judgment to the "Nones"

caught Him by surprise. For this reason, each individual must read His words and decide whether or not to follow Him.

Man Is Accountable

Finally, since God has not been silent, it must be made clear that all people remain personally responsible for their violations of His words. By right of creation, God reserves the power to grant access into His eternal abode or condemn souls to an eternity in hell. Therefore, His words should be viewed as authoritative. He has the right to set the boundary marks in our lives. His commands constitute the standard by which all will be judged in eternity. In modern times, David's confession to Nathan, "I have sinned against the Lord" (2 Sam. 12:13), has been replaced with a myriad of excuses why sinners should be exempt from the guilt of their sin. However, personal guilt must be recognized before forgiveness can be granted. Repentance is the process by which sinners acknowledge their guilt, turn away from their sinful behavior, and seek God's forgiveness. Without sinners accepting the responsibility for their own actions, Jesus's command, "Repent for the kingdom of heaven is at hand" (Matt. 4:17) will never be accomplished, and God's grace will remain out of reach. Without God's grace, standing before Him as a sinner in the Day of Judgment will be an extremely sad and frightening ordeal.

"Nones" may have a concept of God, but they must truly come to know and have confidence in God. The way many in the religious world have twisted the Scriptures may be a stumbling-block, but they must see the need to place their confidence in the inspired word and not in man. Hypocrisy seen in churches may dishearten them, but they still must understand the need to accept personal responsibility for their sins, even if others will not, because God will hold each individual accountable. Answers will have to be given. Eternal destiny will weigh in the balance and they must be prepared.

Conclusion

As Christians seek to evangelize, may Paul's words ever ring in their ears: "Therefore we also have as our ambition, whether at home or absent, to be pleasing to Him. For we must all appear before the judgment seat of Christ, so that each one may be recompensed for his deeds in the body, according to what he has done, whether good or bad. Therefore, knowing the fear of the Lord, we persuade men. . ." (2 Cor. 5:9-11a).

"When Will These Things Be?" : Questions on Eschatology

Bibliography

"Why America's 'Nones' Don't Identify with a Religion." *Pew Research Center.* August 8, 2018. https://www.pewresearch.org/fact-tank/2018/08/08/why-americas-nones-dont-identify-with-a-religion/.

Bible quotations from the *New American Standard Bible: 1995 Update.* La Habra, CA: The Lockman Foundation, 1995.

Is God Cruel to Send Souls to Hell?//
By David A. Cox

Introduction

Many skeptics and atheists claim that God is cruel—pointing to the fact that Scripture teaches that God will judge people and send them to hell. Of course, such a view misunderstands the character of God. In Matthew 25:46, Jesus teaches that there are two destinies where souls will spend eternity after this life: heaven or hell. In the judgment scene that is pictured in Matthew 25, people are judged according to their works, and their destiny is determined by that judgment. Some individuals question the very idea of a place of torment called "hell." They ask, "How could a loving God send people to hell? God is all-knowing. He knows I will make bad choices, so why would He hold that against me? Is that not cruel for God to do that?" Let us consider this thought from what the Scriptures teach about the character of God.

God Is Good

God is wholly good. It is hard for us to even imagine how good He is because, as men, we cannot reach God's heights of goodness. The goodness of God is unequalled. Scripture is filled with affirmations and examples of God's unmatched goodness. A few verses that remind us of His goodness are:

> The Lord is good, a stronghold in the day of trouble; and He knows those who trust in Him (Nah. 1:7).

> Good and upright is the Lord; therefore He teaches sinners in the way (Ps. 25:8).

> Oh, taste and see that the Lord is good; blessed is the man who trusts in Him! (Ps. 34:8).

> Every good gift and every perfect gift is from above, and comes down from the Father of lights, with whom there is no shadow of turning (Jas. 1:17).

"When Will These Things Be?" : Questions on Eschatology

These verses remind us that God only desires what is good for us. Let us remember that every action of God is for the benefit of His people.

God Is Holy and Righteous

"No one is holy like the Lord, For there is none besides You, Nor is there any rock like our God" (1 Sam. 2:2). The holiness of God is without comparison to any. Absolutely no evil is found in God. John said, "God is light; in Him is no darkness at all" (1 John 1:5). The evil impurities and sinful stains that come into our lives are not found with God. It is holiness that leads to the righteousness of God. God is the state of moral perfection. Nothing is lacking in His character that would allow evil to abide. It is perfect righteousness that God required as the atonement for sin. God, knowing man's inability to attain this state, gave His Son to pay the debt that was required for sin (John 3:16).

God Is Loving and Merciful

The love and mercy of God is often the only view men see of God. Sacred Scripture declares, "God is love" (1 John 4:8). The psalmist says, "You, O Lord, are a God full of compassion, and gracious, longsuffering and abundant in mercy and truth" (Ps. 86:15). We see the love and mercy of God in two things:

Seen in the Creation

That God loves us is indisputable. God is the Creator and made everything very good (Gen. 1:31). He put man in the Garden of Eden, a place of perfection, to live and enjoy the abundant blessings there. Adam was not created as a mindless robot, but God allowed him the freedom to choose as he desired. God gave one command "to not eat of the tree of the knowledge of good and evil" (Gen. 2:17). It was Adam and Eve who chose to eat the forbidden fruit, and sin entered the world. God's love was always there, but Adam and Eve's commitment to obeying God was not always present.

Seen in Saving Man

After Adam and Eve sinned, God put them out of the Garden of Eden but began working a plan to save man from sin. The salvation of man involved sending His Son to this earth to pay the penalty for sin: "God demonstrates His own love toward us, in that while we were still sinners, Christ died for us" (Rom. 5:8). The blood of Jesus was shed to redeem man back to God. He still gives man a choice. We can avail our-

Is God Cruel to Send Souls to Hell?

selves of the blood of Jesus, or we can reject it. However, God does not desire that anyone should be lost, but He will force no one to obey Him.

God Is Just

Not only is God good, holy and righteous, loving and merciful—He is also just. God is perfectly upright in the treatment of His creation. He is fair and equitable in His dealings with man. Isaiah writes, "Therefore the Lord will wait, that He may be gracious to you; and therefore He will be exalted, that He may have mercy on you. For the Lord is a God of justice" (Isa. 30:18). God gave commands against the mistreatment of others, and He executes punishment for those that act against the law (Zech. 7:10; Rom. 12:19; 2 Thess. 1:6).

Justice is important to all. That God is a just God is something about which people should be delighted. Divine justice is for our benefit, if we serve Him faithfully. The Hebrew writer states, "For God is not unjust to forget your work and labor of love which you have shown toward His name, in that you have ministered to the saints, and do minister" (Heb. 6:10). The justice and righteousness of God are the foundation of His throne (Ps. 89:14). In this life, individuals may commit hideous crimes, such as rape, murder, assault, etc. What if the guilty party goes before the judge who weighs the evidence, but says, "I know you are guilty of this crime, but I am going to let you go"? Would anyone think that justice had been served? Of course not! Would anyone believe that the judge was cruel if he pronounced the one guilty and gave the most severe penalty that the law allows? No! Why is that the case? Because of justice. We understand that evil acts require punishment. Since creation, all have been given a sense of justice.

Conclusion

God was not cruel to Adam and Eve when they sinned and were cast out of the garden. God was not cruel when He destroyed the world with the flood in Noah's day. We could go on and on with examples of God's judgment and punishment for people committing sin. The fact is that, in every case, God's will was not followed, and they were punished for their transgression. God has always made His will known and expects it to be kept. He gave individuals free choice to do as they want. God loves and cares for all men, but allows them to choose to do as they desire. The same is true today. God's will has been revealed to us. We have the opportunity to consider the things that have been revealed to us. We then must decide either to do God's will or to do our own will. God told us

"When Will These Things Be?" : Questions on Eschatology

that in keeping His will and being righteous, we will be given a home with Him in heaven. God has also said that those who choose not to do His will and practice lawlessness will be cast away from Him into hell, a place of eternal torment.

God is not cruel to send someone to hell who has made the conscious choice not to do His will. Such decisions are made by the individual. God is loving and is not desiring that anyone would be lost, but He will not force one to do something he does not want to do. God is a good, holy, righteous, loving, and merciful God, but He is also a just God and will do what is just and upright.

Creation and the End of the World
By Jim Deason

Introduction
Over the last year, you have often heard someone say, "Just follow the science." That statement contains a measure of truth. For example, with health issues, we need to "follow the science." To maintain good health, we need to follow the instructions of our physicians and nurses. There is a myriad of other ways where that advice makes good practical sense. This is so obviously true that hardly anyone would dispute it.

Still, to be sure, we are confronted with a lot of pseudo-science. These are things that are claimed by scientists as fact and truth when they are not. Let us remember that most of the scientific powers that be—people who tell us to "just follow the science"—do not believe in God, the Bible account of creation, or the concepts of sin and redemption.

Conflicting Worldviews
I am describing two very different worldviews. The one to which we subscribe begins with faith in God, the Bible, and judgment to come. We establish our core values from a foundation of faith. These values determine how we think, what we say, and how we live. To those of us who believe, eternal life and a home with God is in view because death is not the end.

The other worldview begins with a rejection of God and any knowledge of Him. Therefore, since God is now ruled out of the equation, evolution (and not creation) becomes the explanation for the origin of man and the universe in which we live. In the mind of someone who does not believe in God, evolution becomes a *fact* rather than a *theory*. Death is the end of personal existence, dark and foreboding. With this corrupted view of man's beginning and end, the core values that one forms are rooted in faulty human reasoning rather than divine revelation. They are determined by the lowest level of morality that the masses of society will accept. Most modern "science" (as well as the behavior of some on the streets of America today) is founded upon this godless way of thinking. As this anti-God mentality takes control of our educational system, the secular news and entertainment media, and the halls of political power, our culture is becoming increasingly hostile to people of faith. It is impossible that there would be no clash between these two opposing worldviews.

The Christian's Response

So, living in this secular age with faith superseded by "science" in the minds of so many, how is the Christian to react in this environment? Specifically, what does evangelism look like under these conditions? We need men like the ancient sons of Issachar who "understood the times, with knowledge of what Israel should do..." (1 Chron. 12:32). We need *to be such men as these,* equipping ourselves to understand and deal with these changes in our culture and being prepared to make a defense for our hope (cf. 1 Pet. 3:15).

The Foundation of Faith

Let us begin by understanding that there is strong evidence for faith. One man once said that "faith is believing in spite of the evidence." I say faith is believing *because of* the evidence. True science is on the side of the believer. The writer of Hebrews said, "Every house is built by someone, but the builder of all things is God" (Heb. 3:4). Driving past new construction in your community, it's not unusual to ask, "Who is building that house?" Why? Because when you see a building being erected, you know that *someone* is designing and building it. Common sense dictates that design demands a designer. Even someone as simple as I am can see design in the world around me. God is the Great Designer behind the universe in which we live.

The Revelation of God's Mind

It stands to reason that such a God who would design the universe and create man would want to communicate with Him. Sacred Scripture is a record of this communication. The Bible was written by about forty different men from every walk of life, over 1500 years, under almost every conceivable human condition, in three languages, and with a wide variety of literary styles. Yet, it contains such a unity of message that it can only be explained by the fact that a single Divine Mind was behind it all, guiding the writers (1 Cor. 2:12-13; 2 Pet. 1:21). If it is really true that "All Scripture is inspired by God..." (2 Tim 3:16-17)—and it is—then what it records about morality, sin, personal accountability, salvation, and the judgment to come is also true.

This book records the historical narrative of Jesus, the Son of God, who entered the world by virgin birth (Matt. 1:18-25) in fulfillment of prophecy (Isa. 7:14), lived a sinless life (1 Pet. 2:21-22; Heb. 7:26), and out of His love for all mankind gave His life for the sins of the world (Isa. 53; John 3:16; Rom. 5:8). He was "declared the Son of God with power by the resurrection from the dead. . ." (Rom. 1:4). Christ's resurrection stands today as the greatest miracle in human history and the most convincing proof of His deity. Critics may deny His resurrection, but the evidence and veracity of that grand miracle is insurmountable to any reasonable mind and stands as the cornerstone of Christian faith.

Hope vs. Hopelessness

If God is real, and the Bible is His word, and Jesus is His Son, then what the Bible says about Christ's return is also true. Jesus will come again (1 Thess. 4:13-18). When He returns, He will judge all men in righteousness (Matt. 25:31-46; Acts 17:30-31; 2 Cor. 5:10). This world will be destroyed, not by some sort of "green catastrophe" or "nuclear apocalypse," but by divine dictate (2 Pet. 2:10-12).

The hope of the believer is beautifully expressed by the apostle Paul, who said,

> Therefore, we do not lose heart, but though our outer man is decaying, yet our inner man is being renewed day by day. For momentary, light affliction is producing for us an eternal weight of glory far beyond all comparison, while we look not at the things which are seen, but at the things which are not seen; for the things which are seen are temporal, but the things which are not seen are eternal. For we know that if the earthly tent which is our house is torn down, we have a building from God, a house not made with hands, eternal in the heavens (2 Cor. 4:16-5:1).

Conclusion

Here's the thing: Many people in our world, especially unbelievers, are living hopeless and miserable lives. Standing at the graveside of his brother, atheist Robert Ingersoll said, "Life is a narrow vale between the cold and barren peaks of two eternities. We strive in vain to look beyond the heights. We cry aloud, and the only answer is the echo of our wailing cry." Friedrich Nietzsche similarly bemoaned, "Where is my home? For it do I ask and seek, and have sought, but have not found it. O eternal everywhere, O eternal nowhere, O eternal in vain."

Good folks, that is misery! Such statements communicate hopelessness. On the other hand, the good news of Jesus Christ can offer purpose in living and hope in dying. This, I believe, is a message worth believing and worth preaching. This is the only message with the power to convert the world (Mark 16:15-16).

"No One Knows" and the Deity of Christ

By Mike Willis

Introduction

In looking at the various passages related to a study of eschatology, the end-times, some have struggled to reconcile an affirmation of the deity of Jesus with His statement that He did not know the time of His Second Coming. In His sermon on the Mount of Olives regarding the imminent destruction of the city of Jerusalem, Jesus contrasted the destruction of the city which would be preceded by visible signs of its destruction, with the destruction of the heaven and earth, which would not be preceded by visible signs of their destruction. He said:

> Heaven and earth will pass away, but My words will by no means pass away. But of that day and hour no one knows, not even the angels of heaven, but My Father only (Matt. 24:35-36).

> Heaven and earth will pass away, but My words will by no means pass away. But of that day and hour no one knows, not even the angels in heaven, *nor the Son*, but only the Father (Mark 13:31-32).

The Matthean text states that "My Father only" knows the day and hour when the heaven and earth will pass away. In Mark's account, the implication that Jesus does not know that day and hour is explicitly stated by the inclusion of the phrase "nor the Son." This raises the issue of how the Son could not know the day and hour if He were deity. Isn't it the nature of deity to know all things?

Commentaries have struggled to resolve what appears to be a contradiction. During the Arian controversy (third-fourth century AD), an influential heresy denied the deity of Jesus by maintaining that the Son of God was created by the Father and was therefore neither coeternal with the Father, nor consubstantial (of the same essence) with Him.

"When Will These Things Be?" : Questions on Eschatology

Option 1

Those who believe that Jesus was, is, and always will be divine (i.e., He is the Alpha and Omega, Rev. 1:8, 11; 21:6, 13) approach the passage by arguing that Jesus's lack of knowledge about the Second Coming reflected His condition during His incarnation. For example, W. J. Deane (1823-1895) explains that men are excluded from the knowledge of the day and hour, but surely not the Son. He then elaborates that, if the Son were excluded, it was limited to the period when He was incarnate.

> If, then, Christ asserts that he is ignorant of anything, it must be that in his human nature he hath willed not to know that which in his divine nature he was cognizant of (*Pulpit Commentary: The Gospel According to St. Matthew*, 441).

E. Bickersteth (1825-1906) approached the passage in the same way in his comments on Mark 13:32.

> Why, then, does St. Mark here add, "neither the Son"? The answer is surely to be found in the great truth of the hypostatic union. The eternal Son, as God, by his omniscience, and as man, by knowledge imparted to him, knows perfectly the day and the hour of the future judgment. But Christ as man, and as the Messenger from God to men, did not so know it as to be able to reveal it to men. The ambassador, if he is asked concerning the secret counsels of his sovereign, may truly answer that he knows them not so as to communicate them to others. For as an ambassador he only communicates those things which are committed to him by his sovereign to deliver, and not those things which he is bidden to keep secret (*Pulpit Commentary: The Gospel According to St. Mark*, 202).

The great German commentator, H. A. W. Meyer (1800-1873), explained the text in the same way:

> This reservation on the part of the Father excludes even the incarnate Son (Mark 13:32). The limitation implied in our passage as regards the human side of our Lord's nature is to be viewed in the same light as that implied in 20:23 [I'll offer more on this verse later, mw] (*Meyer's Commentary on the New Testament: Matthew*, 427).

Henry Alford (1810-1871) said, "in the course of humiliation undertaken by the Son, in which He increased in wisdom (Luke 2:52), learned obedience (Heb. 5:8), uttered desires in prayer (Luke 6:12, etc.)—*this matter was hidden from Him*" (*The Greek Testament*, I:245).

"No One Knows" and the Deity of Christ

Kyle Pope explained the passage in much the same way, saying, "We must note that this was a statement that Jesus made while (He) was on earth. Whiteside is correct that this 'does not prove that the glorified Christ is now ignorant of that time' (*Doctrinal Discourses*, 298)" (*Truth Commentaries: The Book of Matthew*, 872).

Option 2

Some commentators believe the statement affirms that there are some things the Father knows that are not known by the Son. Leon Morris (1914-2006) stated,

> *That day and hour* defines the measures we use in fixing a date, but that *no one knows* firmly excludes the possibility of doing so. One would have thought that *no one* is definite enough to make clear the impossibility of all date fixing. It shuts out the whole human race from the knowledge in question. But Jesus goes further. *The angels* do not have this knowledge; even in heaven the knowledge is not shared. And what surprises us even more is that *the Son* himself did not share the secret. The only person who knows, Jesus says, is *the Father only*. Nothing could be more explicit (*The Pillar New Testament Commentary: The Gospel according to Matthew*, 613).

One should notice that the context of the statement is one of a high Christology. Jesus speaks of an ascending scale of beings: angels, the Son, and the Father. On this scale, Jesus is above the angels. The doctrine of the deity of Christ is not a late development; Jesus Himself placed Himself above the angels. He is below the Father, not in essence, but in the role which He served. Knowing when the Second Coming would occur is specifically said to be under the control of the Father. Jesus Himself said, "It is not for you to know times or seasons *which the Father has put in His own authority*" [emphasis, mw] (Acts 1:7).

Other passages also show that Jesus served under the will of the Father.

> So He said to them, "You will indeed drink My cup, and be baptized with the baptism that I am baptized with; but to sit on My right hand and on My left is not Mine to give, but it is for those for whom it is prepared by My Father" (Matt. 20:23).

> For "He has put all things under His feet." But when He says "all things are put under Him," it is evident that He who put all things under Him is excepted (1 Cor. 15:27).

251

Both passages recognize a role for the Father that is not given to the Son. I read the statements of Scripture and struggle at times to see how both concepts fit together: Jesus being omnipotent but submissive to the Father; the Holy Spirit being omnipotent but working under the direction of the Father (John 14:16, 26) and Jesus (John 15:26; 16:7, 13). I attribute my struggle to put all the pieces in place to man's limited ability to comprehend the infinite nature of God. The passage so frequently quoted seems applicable here: "The secret things belong to the Lord our God, but those things which are revealed belong to us and to our children forever, that we may do all the words of this law" (Deut. 29:29).

Conclusion

The conclusion which I have reached is to teach what both passages state. Without question, the Bible affirms the deity of Jesus (John 1:1-4, 14; Ps. 45:6 [Heb. 1:8]; Isa. 7:14 [Matt. 1:23]; 9:6; Phil. 2:6; etc.) and there is no question that the Scriptures attribute to the Father some things not affirmed about the Son (Matt. 24:35-35; Mark 13:31-32; Acts 1:7; Matt. 20:23; 1 Cor. 15:27). Whether I fully understand how these things fit together is irrelevant. The entire idea of incarnation strains one's ability to comprehend how Jesus could be fully divine and fully human, but who can deny that this is what the Bible reveals?

Is Matthew 24:34 a Transition Verse?
By Kyle Pope

Among many brethren, a common interpretation of the Olivet Discourse considers Matthew 24:34 a "transition verse" from addressing only the destruction of Jerusalem before it to discussing only final judgment after it. Many see this as a way to avoid the extremes of premillennial views (that imagine a future rebuilt temple and its future destruction) or full-preterist views (that consider the entire discourse as only dealing with the destruction of Jerusalem in AD 70). In this study we will test this interpretation.

If the transition verse view is correct, some compelling language that precedes 24:34 cannot be taken literally but must be interpreted as figurative apocalyptic language describing the significance of God's judgment on Jerusalem. Certainly, Scripture at times uses cosmological end-times language in non-literal ways, but in this case, it presents some challenges I fear some may not have considered.

The Use of Similar Language

Matthew 24:29-33 describes: the sun and moon darkened, stars falling, and the powers of the heavens shaken (24:29), tribes of earth mourning (24:30a), all seeing the Son of Man (30b), the Son of Man coming on clouds (24:30c), coming with power and glory (24:30d), coming with the angels (24:31a), the sound of a trumpet (24:31b), and a gathering for judgment (24:31c). All of these same events are described elsewhere in the New Testament in literal descriptions of Christ's coming in final judgment. For example: Cosmological events (Matt. 5:18; 24:35; Mark 13:31; Luke 21:33; 2 Pet. 3:10, 12; Rev. 20:11; cf. Rev. 21:21), tribes of earth mourning (Rev. 1:7), all seeing Him (Matt. 24:27; Luke 17:24; 1 Cor. 1:7; Col. 3:4; 1 Tim. 6:14; 2 Tim. 4:1, 8; Titus 2:13; 1 Pet. 1:7, 13; Rev. 1:7), the Son of Man coming on clouds (Matt. 26:64; Mark 14:62; Acts 1:9-11; 1 Thess. 4:17; 2 Thess. 2:1; Rev. 1:7), coming with power and glory (Matt. 16:27; 25:31; Mark 8:38; Luke 9:26; cf. Matt. 19:28; 2 Thess. 1:9-10; Col. 3:4; 1 Pet. 1:7; 4:13; 5:1),

"When Will These Things Be?" : Questions on Eschatology

coming with the angels (Matt. 13:41; 16:27; 25:31; Mark 8:38; Luke 9:26; 2 Thess. 1:7; 1 Thess. 4:16), the sound of a trumpet (1 Cor. 15:52; 1 Thess. 4:16), and a gathering for judgment (Matt. 3:12; 13:30, 40, 41; 13:47-48; 16:27; 25:32-33; John 15:6; 2 Thess. 2:1; Rev. 20:12-13).

If these events are literal in other texts why should we take them figuratively in Matthew 24:29-33? If they are figurative in Matthew 24:29-33 why shouldn't we take them figuratively in all of the New Testament? Does their literal application in other texts tell us how New Testament writers interpreted Jesus's words in Matthew 24:29-33? These are important questions to answer. In my understanding, two things lead brethren to this conclusion: (1) how we interpret the phrase "all these things" in 24:34, and (2) how we interpret "immediately" in 24:29.

"All These Things"

Matthew 24:34 reads: "Assuredly, I say to you, this generation will by no means pass away till all these things take place." The argument is that "all these things" must indicate that everything described before this verse must "take place" within the lifetime of the first-century "generation" to whom Jesus was speaking. If this is correct, all the events described in 24:29-33 must be included within the phrase "all these things." We have already seen that this view would demand taking events described in these verses figuratively (of AD 70) that are elsewhere applied literally to Jesus's Second Coming, but there are additional problems with this view.

After Jesus begins to answer the disciples' question, "When will these things be?" (Matt. 24:3b; cf. Mark 13:4a; Luke 21:7b), we often miss that Jesus tells them more about what they would NOT SEE than He does about what they WOULD SEE. Or, more precisely, He tells them what they would see that would not signal "the end" and what they would see that would demand action. Notice, He tells them that they must, "take heed (*blepō*) that no one deceives you" (24:4b). The Greek word *blepō* means "to see, discern, of the bodily eye" (Thayer). It is one of several words in Greek that describe vision. Let's notice the emphasis throughout this section on what He said they would and would not "see."

In 24:5-12, He tells them they would see: false christs (24:5), wars and rumors of wars (24:6a), conflict between nations and kingdoms (24:7a), famines, pestilences, and earthquakes (24:7b), persecution and hatred towards Christians (24:9), stumbling, betrayal, and hatred (24:10), false

Is Matthew 24:34 a Transition Verse?

prophets (24:11), and falling away (24:12). Yet, He tells them these things were not to be interpreted as "the end" (24:6b). It is not until 24:15-22 that He first tells them of anything they could expect to "see" that relates to any portion of their question and upon which they should act. He declares, "Therefore when YOU SEE the 'abomination of desolation,'... then let those who are in Judea FLEE to the mountains" (24:15-16, emphasis mine). It is this event that He calls an unparalleled time of "great tribulation" (24:21). There is no question that this is talking about AD 70. After this, in 24:23-28 He returns to warning them again not to be deceived, again spelling out what they would see and what they would not see.

There are many reasons why I reject the AD 70 Doctrine with its false conclusion that the Lord's Second Coming was accomplished in AD 70. But, one big reason is because verse 23 tells me not to! Notice: "Then"— when? At AD 70, at the time of the "great tribulation." Jesus says, then "If anyone says to you, 'Look, here is the Christ'... DO NOT BELIEVE IT" (emphasis mine). Jesus says not to believe claims that say, "Here is Christ, in the events of AD 70!" Does that only apply to claims made by those living during AD 70? No. Does it only apply to false christs that pretended to be Christ in AD 70? No. He even addresses the unseen claims: "Therefore if they say to you, 'Look, He is in the desert!' do not go out; or 'Look, He is in the inner rooms!' DO NOT BELIEVE IT" (24:26, emphasis mine). To argue that AD 70 was the second and final coming of Jesus is a direct contradiction of the Lord's commands in Matthew 24:23! It would have us believe that "then," although many other false christs came whom they should reject, we should believe at least one claim that says, "Here is the Christ, in the events of AD 70." I can't do that!

To accept this view, we also have to ignore His very next words: "For as the lightning comes from the east and flashes to the west, so also will the coming (*parousia*) of the Son of Man be" (24:27). Lightning is unmistakable. Everyone sees it. Even those sitting in a house will see the flash from "east" to "west." The very fact that we still discuss whether AD 70 was the "coming (*parousia*)" of Jesus shows that it could not have been! Jesus says that when it happens, like lightning, it will be unmistakable. The fourth-century preacher John Chysostom, a native of Syrian Antioch, to whom ancient Greek was his native language, wrote of this passage:

"When Will These Things Be?" : Questions on Eschatology

How then doth He Himself come? "As the lightning cometh out of the east, and shineth even unto the west, so shall also the coming of the Son of Man be"... How then shineth the lightning? It needs not one to talk of it, it needs not a herald, but even to them that sit in houses, and to them in chambers it shows itself in an instant of time throughout the whole world. So shall that coming be, showing itself at once everywhere by reason of the shining forth of His glory (*Homily* 76, on Matt. 24:16-18.3).

In material presented in the companion volume of this study guide I discussed the focus of the Olivet Discourse. I explored the meaning and use of the word *parousia*, translated "coming" in this verse and elsewhere in the New Testament. I argue that by using this word Jesus could not have chosen a term that makes it any clearer that His coming would involve an actual, literal, visible, presence of Jesus Christ that, like His first coming, will also be an actual, literal, visible, presence (see 2 Pet. 1:16). That did not happen in AD 70! To argue otherwise is to take a word with no demonstrable Biblical or extra-biblical examples of being used in a figurative or representative manner and force a meaning upon it that is foreign to its use in ancient Greek.

How then should we understand the scope of the phrase "all these things" in 24:34? The verse right before it says, "So you also, when you SEE ALL THESE THINGS, know that it is near—at the doors!" (24:33, emphasis mine). He is talking about things they could "see," or see that would not signal the end. He is not talking about things they would not (or could not) see. Again, what would they see? False christs (24:5), wars and rumors of wars (24:6a), conflict between nations and kingdoms (24:7a), famines, pestilences, and earthquakes (24:7b), persecution and hatred towards Christians (24:9), stumbling, betrayal, and hatred (24:10), false prophets (24:11), and falling away (24:12), but these things were not to be interpreted as "the end" (24:6b). They would "see" the "Abomination of Desolation," or as Luke explains, "But when YOU SEE Jerusalem surrounded by armies, then know that its desolation is near" (Luke 21:20, emphasis mine). When they saw this, they were to "flee." These are the things He says they would "see," not the events of 24:29-33.

I fear that brethren have overlooked a major problem this creates. The transition verse view must argue that the events of 24:29-33 were fulfilled in an unseen figurative way in AD 70, but it must also include

Is Matthew 24:34 a Transition Verse?

them within "all these things" in 24:34. The problem is Jesus says "all these things" are things they would "see" (24:33), so unseen things cannot be included within "all these things" if they could not be seen. We can't have it both ways.

The Use of "Immediately" in 24:29

Matthew 24:29 begins, "Immediately (*eutheōs*) after the tribulation of those days" (NKJV), and then describes apocalyptic events associated with the coming of the Son of Man (24:29b-33). The argument is that the Greek word *eutheōs*, translated "immediately," demands that there could be little or no time interval between the "tribulation f those days" (i.e. AD 70), and the coming of Jesus in the next verses. For the transition verse view to be correct, it must be proven that the force of *eutheōs* is so conclusive that there can be no question that it connects the "Abomination of Desolation" (24:15) and the time of "great tribulation" (24:21) with the "Son of Man coming on the clouds" (24:30). On the other hand, if *eutheōs* is a relative term that can apply to different time intervals it does not demand that we interpret 24:29-33 figuratively.

Small or Straight?

There is no question that this word is often applied to time intervals that are very small. The question is whether the intrinsic meaning of *eutheōs* carries sufficient force to nullify a literal interpretation of 24:29-33 by other New Testament writers and to include these yet unseen events within the scope of "all these things" which Jesus said that generation would "see" (24:33-34). A flaw in this reasoning assumes that the conceptual basis of *eutheōs* is *smallness*. That leads to the assumption that when applied to time or sequence the issue is the span of time. That is incorrect. In fact, the conceptual basis of it is *straightness*, so when applied to time the span of time can vary, but the directness in relation to sequence or importance is what is emphasized. To treat this word as if it is a precise measurement of something small is a misunderstanding of its full scope.

This can be seen from the foremost Lexicon of the ancient Greek language, *A Greek-English Lexicon*, by Henry George Liddell and Robert Scott, revised by Sir Henry Stuart Jones (Oxford: Clarendon Press, 1940)—usually abbreviated LSJ. This lexicon is not concerned with promoting a religious perspective, but solely focuses on word meaning as demonstrated in Classical, Hellenistic, and Koine Greek (ca. 700 BC –

AD 500). The entry for this word and the word from which it is derived is available online.[1]

A survey of its entry in LSJ shows that *eutheōs* is an adverbial form of *euthus*, and both words can be used interchangeably with the same meaning. The first, and primary definition of *euthus*, with documented sources, reads (A) "*straight, direct,* whether vertically or horizontally, as opposed to *skolios* [curved], *kampulos* [bent]." It was used of the vertical of a spinning top, of a straight road (as in Acts 9:11, "Straight Street" and Matt. 3:3, Mark 1:3, and Luke 3:4-5 of "straight paths"). It referred to going straight forward, in a direct line, or on the same side. The second portion of the entry, explaining its use in a moral sense, reads (2) "*straightforward, frank,* to speak *straight out, outright, openly, without reserve, by direct reasoning.*" From this we see that its moral sense is derived from its primary conceptual basis of *straightness*. We cannot look at the entire entry in this study, but we should note that in a metaphorical sense *euthus* can mean, "*at once, naturally.*" It can be used of manner: (3) "*directly, simply*" and (4) in the sense of "*for instance, to take the first example that occurs.*" This demonstrates that while the conceptual basis of this word is the straightness of something, at times it serves a narrative function simply pointing to the next thing in the story with little or no connection to the time involved.

The final two sections of the LSJ entry (C) deal specifically with the adverb *eutheōs*. It begins by explaining that it is "used just as *euthus.*" That tells us that all that is said about *euthus* applies equally to this form of the word. It cites examples such as, "*as soon as* he perceived" and "since he breathed out *immediately.*" The final subsection (2) repeats that *eutheōs* "= *euthus*" showing an example of it with the word *oion* [such as] to mean "*as for example.*" It also explains that "*eutheōs* is the commoner form in later Greek," which is significant for our discussion of Biblical Greek.

Biblical Usage

The use of *eutheōs* and *euthus* in the Septuagint (LXX), the Greek OT produced before the first century, and the Greek NT attest that many (if not all) of the applications cited from LSJ are attested in Biblical Greek.

---

[1] http://www.perseus.tufts.edu/hopper/text?doc=Perseus%3Atext%3A1999.04.0057%3Aentry%3Deu)qu%2Fs

Is Matthew 24:34 a Transition Verse?

Often *euthus* is used of the "straight road" or path. For example, "The voice of one crying in the wilderness: 'Prepare the way of the LORD; make straight (*euthus*) in the desert a highway for our God. Every valley shall be exalted and every mountain and hill brought low; The crooked places shall be made straight (*euthus*) and the rough places smooth'" (Isa. 40:3-4; cf. 42:16; Matt. 3:3; Mark 1:3; Luke 3:4-5; Acts 13:10; et al.). This frequent usage demonstrates that however we understand the application of *eutheōs* (and *euthus*) to time the conceptual basis literally refers to the straightness of something.

Specific New Testament Examples

When applied to time, how are these words used in the New Testament? Examples of both *eutheōs* and *euthus* clearly show them to be relative terms that can apply to different time intervals.

The Parable of the Sower. In the Parable of the Sower, it is used in reference to the seed sown on stony places that "immediately (*eutheōs*) sprang up" (Matt. 13:5). Obviously, some time was involved between sowing and springing up.

"See You Shortly." In 3 John 14, John uses *eutheōs* (translated "shortly") of his desire to come to the brethren and see them "face to face." This does not set a specific measure of time (such as "in two years" or "in the spring") but a relative and variable time interval. The context here, obviously, limits the time interval intended by *eutheōs* because John and the brethren to whom he wrote both had limited lifespans. What if John and the brethren had lived for centuries (as the patriarchs once did)? Would that extend the interval of the term "shortly (*eutheōs*)" to a lifespan of centuries? Yes. What if one of the parties in such a statement was God (possessing an unlimited lifespan)? Would that not extend the interval allowed by the term "shortly (*eutheōs*)" even further? Yes. That is exactly the circumstance in Matthew 24-25. Jesus (who is eternal in nature) describes times and seasons to mortal man.

The Parable of the Talents. In Matthew 25:15-16, in the Parable of the Talents, *eutheōs* comes at either the end of 24:15 or the beginning of 24:16. This is why the editors of the KJV (and NKJV) have the master leaving "immediately," while the NASB (and other translations) say of the five talent man, "immediately the one who had received the five talents went and traded with them, and gained five more talents." Would

"When Will These Things Be?" : Questions on Eschatology

there be various intervals in how long it would take the master to leave, the servant to go (or if we can extend "immediately" to his trading and gaining "five more talents")? Yes. Clearly, *eutheōs* is a relative term, not a set measurement of time.

"Long Time." Some have argued that since *eutheōs* is not applied to the master's return in the Parable of the Talents, we cannot understand the use of *eutheōs* in Matthew 24:29 to allow for a "long time" between the time of "great tribulation" and the "Son of Man coming on the clouds." But let's think about this for a minute. The Parable of the Talents (Matt. 25:14-30) comes within the same discourse as Matthew 24:29-33. The majority of Greek manuscripts, just before its beginning read, "Watch therefore, for you know neither the day nor the hour in which the Son of Man is coming" (25:13, NKJV), and then continue, "For it is just like a man about to go on a journey" (25:14a, NASB). That shows us that the coming of the Son of Man is "just like" a man who goes on a journey. Right after this parable, Jesus continues, "When the Son of Man comes in His glory, and all the holy angels with Him, then He will sit on the throne of His glory" (25:31, NKJV). This is a parable about Jesus's coming! And yet, when it describes the interval between the master's departure and his return it calls it "a long time" (25:19). Jesus uses the phrase "long time" in a similar way in another parable He told on the same day as the Olivet Discourse during His extended teaching within the temple (see Luke 20:1-8; cf. Matt. 21:23-27). We call it the Parable of the Wicked Vinedressers (Luke 20:9-19). It begins, "Then He began to tell the people this parable: 'A certain man planted a vineyard, leased it to vinedressers, and went into a far country for a LONG TIME" (Luke 20:9, emphasis mine). So, twice, on the same day (and once in this same discourse) Jesus describes the interval between planting and harvest, or the interval representing His own departure and return as a "long time."

"Glorify Him Immediately." In John 13:32. Jesus says, "If God is glorified in Him, God will also glorify Him in Himself, and glorify Him immediately (*euthus*)." This wording challenges a rigid limitation of the term "immediately." To what and to when was this immediate glorification pointing? In John 13:31 Jesus described His glorification as a present condition, but in Acts 3:12-15 Peter connected the glorification of Jesus with what God did in Christ's resurrection. In 2 Thessalonians 1:10, how-

Is Matthew 24:34 a Transition Verse?

ever, Paul connects it with "when He comes, in that Day, to be glorified in His saints and to be admired among all those who believe." Is this a future Second Coming? If so, "glorify Him immediately" spans an interval of centuries. Full-preterists argue that this "Day" refers to AD 70. If so, "glorify Him immediately" would at least span from AD 33 to AD 70. Regardless of how we understand John 13:32 it proves that *euthus* is a relative term that can apply to different intervals of time.

A Narrative Device. Johannes Weiss, in a study he did on the use of *euthus* in Mark, demonstrated that there are times when this word has nothing to do with time. Weiss argued that comparisons between the use of *euthus* in Mark with parallels in Matthew and Luke reveal clear examples of its use as a narrative marker similar to the Hebrew construction known as the waw-consecutive. This grammatical form is often translated "and so" or "therefore." For example, Mark 15:1a reads, "Immediately (*euthus*), in the morning, the chief priests held a consultation with the elders and scribes and the whole council." Matthew, however, puts this, "When morning came, all the chief priests and elders of the people plotted against Jesus to put Him to death" (Matt. 27:1). Luke reads, "Then the whole multitude of them arose and led Him to Pilate" (Luke 23:1). All three are describing the same event, but only Mark uses *euthus*. In Mark, *euthus* stands parallel to "when" (in Matthew) and "then" (in Luke).[2] This suggests that *euthus* does not always imply haste but sometimes just points to the next thing being related in the narrative. If Weiss is correct, the idea in Matthew 24:29 may have nothing to do with the span of time until the Lord's coming, it may be used as a narrative device, to express, "and so, after the tribulation of those days...."

All of these examples demonstrate that *eutheōs* and *euthus* are relative terms that can be applied to different time intervals. So, in Matthew 24:29 there is no intrinsic reason to conclude from the use of *eutheōs* that it forces us to disregard literal interpretations of the events in 24:29-33 by other New Testament writers or to overlook the fact that Jesus said they would actually "see all these things." *Eutheōs* is a relative term that can

---

2 Johannes Weiss, "ΕΥΘΥΣ bei Markus [*Euthus* in Mark]," *Zeitschrift für die neutestamentliche Wissenschaft und die Kunde der älteren Kirche* [*Journal of New Testament Science and Education from the Early Church*] 11.2 (1910): 124-133.

apply to different time intervals, and even to situations where time is not the issue involved in its use.

"After," Not at the Same Time

The transition verse view must argue that *eutheōs* in Matthew 24:29 demands that we understand it to connect the events associated with the "Abomination of Desolation" and the "great tribulation" with the events described in 24:29-33. This conclusion overlooks the fact that this is consistently qualified as something that happens "after" those events. Parallel accounts demonstrate the same fact. Mark writes, "But in those days, after that tribulation, the sun will be darkened, and the moon will not give its light" (Mark 13:24). Mark is describing the days "after that tribulation" (regardless of when they would occur). He is not equating the two. Luke's use of "immediately" is especially enlightening. He writes, "But when you hear of wars and commotions, do not be terrified; for these things must come to pass first, but the end will not come immediately (*eutheōs*)" (Luke 21:9, NKJV) or as the NASB reads, "And when you hear of wars and disturbances, do not be terrified; for these things must take place first, but the end does not follow immediately (*eutheōs*)." Does Luke's use of "immediately" automatically identify it with the same focus as Matthew 24:29? No! If so, Luke is contradicting Matthew. Instead, Luke says "the end" will not come immediately, whereas Matthew describes the sequence of the tribulation in relation to the later (and still future) coming of the Son of Man.

"This Generation"

Finally, some have argued that the promises regarding punishment of those who shed innocent blood (Matt. 23:36), and that those living would "not taste death" until the kingdom came (Luke 9:27; Mark 9:1; Matt. 16:28) set a limit on the time interval implied in the use of *eutheōs*. But this assumes it must apply to time and ignores the arguments we have already made. Yes, the generation living at the time would "see" the visible things Jesus said they could see. Yet, if Jesus came in AD 70 all of the evens of 24:29-33 were unseen. No one saw them, especially "all the tribes of the earth" whom Jesus said would "SEE the Son of Man coming on the clouds" (24:30, emphasis mine)! So, the promises Jesus made to that "generation" have no bearing on how we interpret the time interval involved in the use of *eutheōs* in Matthew 24:29. It remains a relative term that can apply to different intervals of time. To demand that *eutheōs*

Is Matthew 24:34 a Transition Verse?

requires that the events of 24:29-33 had to take place within the lifespan of the "generation" living at the time Jesus spoke is a forced and arbitrary conclusion that does not fit the context or the different applications of this word in ancient Greek.

Authors of Essays in the Companion Text

Big Questions

What Is Eternal Life and Why Should It Matter to Me?
Tommy Peeler

What Does the Bible Teach about Hell and Who Will Go There?
Ron Halbrook

Am I Ready for the End?
Bobby Graham

The Kingdom

Has the Kingdom of Christ Been Established?
Joe Price

Does the Physical Nation of Israel Still Play a Role in God's Final Plans?
Stephen Russell

Can Signs Foretell When the End Will Come?
Allen Dvorak

Judgment Day

What Does the Bible Teach about the Coming of Christ?
Kevin Kay

What Is the Biblical Teaching on the Resurrection?
Bruce Reeves

Does the Bible Teach the "Rapture," the Coming of an Antichrist, and the Battle of Armageddon?
Mark Mayberry

Tough Questions

Does the Bible Teach an End of This Universe?
Chris Reeves

Authors of Essays in the Companion Text

What Is the Focus of the Mount of Olives Discourse?
Kyle Pope

When Was Revelation Written and Why Does It Matter?
Daniel H. King, Sr.

Personal Eschatology: Men's Studies

Where Are the Dead?
Jesse Flowers

Does the Bible Teach Purgatory?
Daniel and Diana Dow

Does the Bible Teach Reincarnation?
Steve Wallace

Personal Eschatology: Women's Studies

Where Are the Dead?
Aleta Samford

Does the Bible Teach Purgatory?
Daniel and Diana Dow

Does the Bible Teach Reincarnation?
Jennifer Maxey

Appendix: General Studies

Premillennialism
Mike Willis

Postmillennialism
David Dann

Amillennialism
Sean Cavender

The New Heavens and New Earth
Jim McDonald

The AD 70 Doctrine
Don McClain

Eco-Eschatology
Matthew Bassford

What Does the Bible Teach about Hades and Sheol?
Kyle Pope

www.ingramcontent.com/pod-product-compliance
Lightning Source LLC
Chambersburg PA
CBHW070758230426
43665CB00017B/2404